DARK
NOSTALGIA

DARK NOSTALGIA

Faultlessly Stylish Interiors for Business, Pleasure and Leisure

EVA HAGBERG

First published in the United Kingdom in 2009 by
Thames & Hudson Ltd, 181A High Holborn,
London WC1V 7QX

www.thamesandhudson.com

British Library Cataloguing-in-Publication Data
A catalogue record for this book is available from the British Library

ISBN: 978-0-500-51509-9

Printed and bound in China

This book has been a collaboration in many ways. I am grateful to the following people, and many more:

Andrea Monfried, who took me to lunch and suggested I write a book, then gently shepherded my kernel of an idea through to fruition. Stacee Lawrence, whose remarkable dedication, focus, and care has been matched only by her immeasurable improvements. Claudia Brandenburg, who translated a pile of words and a pile of images into a design that not only perfectly expresses my thoughts, but adds new layers of meaning I hadn't even imagined.

Martin Pedersen and Kristi Cameron at *Metropolis* were among the first to lend me a forum, and continue to keep me on track, in line, and writing. My editors at *Wallpaper∗*, particularly Nick Compton and Richard Cook, have given me more than enough time, space, and gentle guidance with which to figure out how to write about architecture. Thank you.

William Bostwick: thank you for your encouragement, your friendship, and for lending me the best line in the book. Thanks also to John Powers, whose edits, conversations, and enthusiasm brought a profound clarity to the project's murky early days, and to Philip Nobel, for teaching me so much.

Special thanks as well to: Paola Antonelli, Gillian Bostock, Sophie Donelson, Rosalie Genevro, Liz Kubany, Chani Lisbon, Roy McMakin, David Rueger, Andrea Schwan, Chaya Simon, Davey Volner, and Bill and Martha Wilson.

And, of course, every designer and photographer whose work appears in these pages, as well as the owners, who were so enthusiastic about participating. Your generosity and support mean everything to me, and it wouldn't be a book—or an idea—without you.

INTRODUCTION

When the Royalton Hotel renovation was unveiled in New York in the fall of 2007, it marked the end of an era. It was also a public marker of the beginnings of another, one that had been simmering. Gone were Philippe Starck's playful-philosophical chairs. Gone were the round shapes and cartoonish forms, relics of a design time that thrived on words like "blobby," "organic," and "computer." Gone were the jokes, the puns, the inside references.

There, now, was a hand-forged fireplace grate, a wrapped metal screen, fur. There, at this Manhattan media hotspot, were spun rope nets, polished wood banquettes, deep heavy colors. The architects of the renovation, Roman and Williams, had so thoroughly removed Starck, had so completely stamped their own gritty and dark nostalgia onto the place, that critics didn't know what to do. Some mourned the loss of an icon. Others complained about the materials. Mostly, they didn't know what to say.

As it turns out, we weren't losing an icon. We were being offered a new one. While the Royalton's designers, Roman and Williams, were working, other establishments with a similar sensibility were cropping up as well. Allen & Delancey, for example, a brick-walled, book-lined, velvet-curtained restaurant, opened on New York's Lower East Side and served dishes like marrow bones, boiled beef, and scallops with cream. In Paris, a seventeenth-century building was transformed with slick all-black walls, and in San Francisco, a former speakeasy reintroduced the use of the password for entry.

The projects that follow show that we have become nostalgic for a time that never existed. They demonstrate, through this re-creation of history's deep colors, polished woods, velvets, furs, leather, and burnished metals, that we would rather live by creating our present through an imagination of our past. We love these dark materials for their ability to evoke emotions and moods, for their warmth and acceptance of the somber sides of life. We are re-creating our own history and embracing the darkness that comes with it.

I have never been one to get homesick. I have never thought things would be better if only I were somewhere else, or that they had been better when I had been somewhere else. I accepted everywhere I was, while I was there. In retrospect, some situations were better, some worse, but I found a way to be as happy in a slant-floored Upper East Side rental apartment as I had been in my family home. I never secretly hoped that things would return to the way they had been. And so I believed I was nostalgia-immune.

Many of the projects featured here are places I know well, and their architecture, design, and aesthetic affected the way my friends, colleagues, and I began to craft and then live our professional lives. With as much personality as the individuals who created them, they called us back time and again with their bold and fantastically self-indulgent embrace of purposeful alteration, decadent taste, and sometimes, pure play.

Bars and restaurants are bounded spaces; while they offer moments of happiness and excitement and possibility, the experience is nevertheless framed, controlled. When we visit these hotels, restaurants, and bars, we enter into their creators' worlds—publicly articulated through the menu selection or the design of a table or a chair. These spaces give us a chance to travel through time, allowing us—even if only temporarily—to experience firsthand how freeing the original versions of these places must have been in societies that were much more strict than ours.

The first time I ate at Freemans, a tiny restaurant hidden at the end of an obscure alley, what I immediately felt was the promise of a future in which, surrounded by relics from the past, I would be able to remember this dinner as the first in a line of many. It was the same with the Stanton Social and with Public. I lived around the corner from the Bowery Hotel while it was under construction, but ended up moving before it opened. It was a year before I was able to return and spend an evening in its Havana-inspired lobby, and the hotel's weighty, permanent atmosphere, coupled with my own memories of anticipating its opening, amplified my nostalgia.

These experiences made me realize that I am not immune. I do get nostalgic. But the nostalgia is often about an imagined or future time, created by these spaces' emotional immediacy. An instant nostalgia for a time with clear rules about appropriate behavior comes up at Employees Only, while another nostalgia, for the fearless, even self-destructive experimentation of a more decadent moment, is sated by Death & Company, and still another, perhaps for the oblivion of opium dens, by Apothéke. The approaches differ, but each establishment shares a commonality of intent—to create a space that offers an immediate continuity between the present and the imagined future, the idealized past and today. The narratives of our lives become public when played out on the stage of a restaurant or a bar, acted out in the theater of dinner or drinks. A constant interrelationship between designed visual cues such as torn wallpaper or an abstracted herringbone pattern in glass cause us to act differently in each place.

In private spaces, such as the Mazeau Lyons house and the Robin Standefer and Stephen Alesch NoHo apartment and Montauk house, design cues are less overtly polemical, more personal, but they share the same sense of stagecraft, of architectural and design theater. As I told Alesch and Standefer during my first visit to their loft, it was the kind of place I wish I would be able to look back on having lived in. Here, in a home, the intimacy inherent in the act of architectural creation is most apparent. Without reveling in a new conservatism or a desire to pretend that they actually stumbled into these houses and merely added a few contemporary touches here and there, their work is self-aware, purposeful, and, through its success at producing a mood before an abstracted thought, profound.

Good architecture and interior design influence us by inspiring an immediate emotional connection, an evocation more than a linear thought process. As much as we tell stories about ourselves through language and articulation, so too do we create narratives and belief systems through floorboards and kitchen layouts. An immediacy and urgency of emotional response connects these interiors. None of them operates without the continued presence of their owners, their designers, and their visitors. They haven't been designed from a distance or conceived from far away. They are intensely personal, romanticized and real, idealized and made manifest, and saturated with memory—the owners', the designers', mine.

All the places featured have some tug, some pull. It is impossible to walk into spaces like these and not immediately relate, not shape any criticism or understanding of them around the currency of our past and right-now lives. As a student, I willed myself to believe in a neutral formal-ism—a true shape cut away from the arbitrary forms of the past, an angle that would save the world. I wanted to design buildings that were about completely abstracted and formalist ideas, wished I could be more like Mies, but I found myself truly drawn to spaces that made me feel.

Architecture is at once the most intimate artistic practice there is, and the most general. On the most basic level, we put our bodies into buildings, and on a more philosophical level, our minds accompany them. We acknowledge that the experience could change us, but the means are ever-mutable. Some architecture is about the future, about bombastic moves that offer clarity, or excitement, or a promise that the world will be different—and in the coolest way. But the architecture here does the opposite.

The layering of history that we see in these spaces, the weight with which so many of them have been considered and designed, immedi-ately reassures us that our today—even once we've left the cocooned surroundings of dark wood and detailed chandeliers and stuffed eagles and weighty whale bones—is going to be better than all right. This brief dip in the sea of memory calms our turbulent present and reminds us that soon, this moment too shall be the past. At several of these places, I still find it difficult to walk in the doors and not feel immediately suf-fused with a romanticized notion of an earlier life plan, long since aban-doned. This collection of knotty planks and rococo mirrors and reclaimed lights and ancient fan belts have all come together to paint a picture of a time that never was, but still a time that I can remember wanting.

The dark nostalgia here is bittersweet. I do not long for things, persons, or situations of the past, but I have longed to be able to accept them in my present. These spaces, and the architecture and design found within them, show that not only is it possible to be an amalgam of all that has come before, but also that it is possible to find coherence in a mixed-up idealization of a vague conception of the past, and that it is desirable to acknowledge desire. We read these material cues, these palettes, and we are reassured. This architecture shows that we can love our past and our longing. And it shows us how to live.

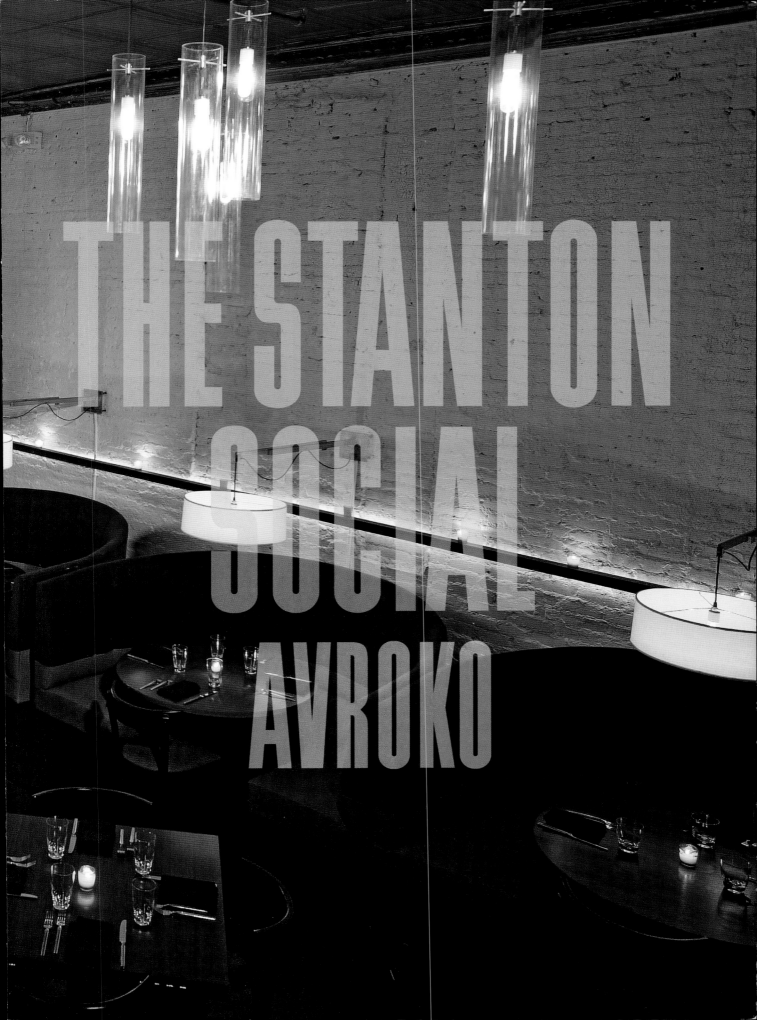

THE STANTON SOCIAL

AVROKO

Before Manhattan's Lower East Side became a haven for the hipster fashionista set, and long before it became an epicenter of banking money and glass-tower architecture, the neighborhood was home to the city's original garment district, full of tailors and seamstresses. Half a century after the neighborhood ceded its identity to Seventh Avenue, AvroKO principal Kristina O'Neal saw that telling the history of the haberdashers long gone—and honoring the industry's remnants that can still be glimpsed in certain storefronts—by translating them into design was a natural fit.

The architects deconstructed dozens of vintage suits in search of inspiring forms and compelling structure, and as a result, the restaurant is built with the same level of sophistication as a bespoke 1940s waistcoat. Its design is also similarly based in function as much as in ornament. The Stanton Social name serves as a reminder of a time when "socials" were activities, and the restaurant adopts their convivial mood while simultaneously evoking the propriety of their era.

The space is neatly divided. Downstairs in the bar, beltlike leather details conjure a connection to the neighborhood's past. Exposed brick walls serve as a physical reminder that the site has a long memory, and the use of dark materials and woods throughout creates bold details associated with a masculine space.

If the downstairs is a men's club, the upstairs is a boudoir. The aesthetic moves from the heaviness associated with a chunky wool suit—referenced by a wall of shelves whose lines create a herringbone pattern—to more ethereal decorations. On the second floor, the lampshades swoop out, mimicking a skirt, a corset, or a woman's hips. Here, shapes and furnishings are sensual. A pattern of cherry blossoms floats across the striated walls, their reaching branches contrasting completely with the strong, defined space below. Every design element iterates the firm's ultimate intent: to remind diners of the site's sartorial past.

(above)
HISTORICAL ORNAMENTS INCORPORATED IN A MODERN WAY GRACE THIS GLOWING,
RED BATHROOM SPACE

(previous pages)
ROUND LAMPS JUT OUT FROM ORIGINAL BRICK WALLS TO OVERHANG DEEPLY
CURVED, DARK BANQUETTES; THE STARK CONTRAST AND USE OF CLUBBY MATERIALS
CREATES A MASCULINE SPACE

(above)
BLOCKY BROWN LEATHER SOFAS ARE DETAILED WITH STRAPPED-AND-
BUCKLED-IN PILLOWS; ART DISPLAYING OVERSIZED STITCHING LIKE THAT
FOUND ON CLOTHING LABELS REFERENCES THE NEIGHBORHOOD'S
GARMENT-DISTRICT PAST

(opposite)
LEATHER STRAPS ADD TEXTURE TO THE STAIRCASE AND UNITE THE
ARCHITECTURE WITH THE RESTAURANT'S THEME

(above)
PORTHOLE-LIKE MIRRORS, HIGHLY POLISHED WOODS, AND STREAMLINED CHAIRS
EVOKE A 1940S OCEAN LINER

(opposite)
WINE BOTTLES NESTLE TOGETHER IN A SERIES OF GEOMETRIC SHELVES
WHOSE LINES CREATE A HERRINGBONE PATTERN MEANT TO EVOKE A MAN'S SUIT;
A SPARSELY SUPPORTED STAIRCASE, ALL THIN CABLES AND ARTICULATED
RISERS, INDICATES A SHIFT IN SCALE FROM THE MASCULINE DOWNSTAIRS SPACE
TO THE FEMININE UPSTAIRS

(above)
ON THE SECOND FLOOR, CURVED LAMPSHADES AND A PATTERN OF
CHERRY BLOSSOMS LIKE THOSE FOUND ON FINE SILKS CREATE A DISTINCTLY
FEMININE SPACE

(opposite)
ROWS OF OLD-FASHIONED LAMPS WITH FRITTED GLASS SHADES LEAD
UPSTAIRS, LIGHTING THE DARK WOOD STEPS AND HIGHLIGHTING THE DETAIL IN
THE PRESSED TIN CEILING

THE BOWERY HOTEL

SEAN MACPHERSON
ERIC GOODE

Part of the construction boom that turned its immediate neighborhood, once infamous for drugs and flophouses, into a streetscape lined with restaurants and luxury condominium housing, the Bowery Hotel opened in Manhattan in 2007. Its dark wood, Havana-inspired aesthetic immediately announced the beginning of a new, alternate history to a neighborhood swimming in its own.

Owner and designer Sean MacPherson felt that many of the quickly encroaching glass towers lacked soul and a connection to the past. Recognizing that his hotel, an admittedly indulgent space, would open right next door to a still-functioning homeless shelter, he decided to carefully balance historical elements with overt change. Even though the design evokes Cuba, it was important to him that the structure also maintain a palpably New York aura. "We referenced downtown loft and industrial buildings, and also prewar apartments that feel solid and comfortable, and even a little bit conservative in a way," he says.

MacPherson was inspired by the Algonquin Hotel in Midtown, known for its long history of famous literary guests, as a similarly low-trend but high-comfort establishment. To achieve the exact aesthetic they wanted, he and his partners personally selected every single rug and object in the Bowery's lobby and bar. To differentiate his space from contemporary buildings springing up nearby, he focused on creating depth, incorporating weighty materials such as solid wood, real stone, and old hinges—and by trusting his instinct.

"There's something very reassuring about a place that you know was there long before you and that will be there long after you," MacPherson says, explaining the pull of history. "There's a comfort in nostalgia." The Bowery Hotel is a completely renovated building, but one that successfully exudes the sense of permanence normally associated with older structures. It feels as though it has been there for decades, making you wonder how you never noticed it before.

(above)
A SPARELY OUTFITTED GUEST ROOM OFFERS A SUBTLE INTERPRETATION OF THE
HOTEL'S HAVANA-INSPIRED AESTHETIC

(previous pages)
AN ARCHWAY HUNG WITH A DOUBLE SET OF VELVET CURTAINS LEADS TO THE
HOTEL'S MAIN BAR; ITS BROCADE WALLPAPER IS SET OFF BY ORNATE SCONCES, DARK
WAINSCOTING, MOUNTED ANTLERS, AND A MIRRORED CEILING

(overleaf)
WICKER CHAIRS, ORNATELY PATTERNED CARPETS AND UPHOLSTERY, ELABORATE
TILE WORK, POTTED PALMS, AND A DECORATIVELY PAINTED WOODEN CEILING CREATE
A CUBAN MOOD IN THE EVENT SPACE

A DETAILED FIREPLACE WITH A POINTED ARCH PROVIDES THE PERFECT BACKDROP
TO ORNATELY CARVED CHAIRS AND INTRICATE WROUGHT-IRON BENCHES WITH
INVITING GREEN VELVET SEATS. MURALS DEPICTING THE BROOKLYN BRIDGE ADD A
LAYER OF HISTORICAL REFERENCE TO THE ROOM

FURNISHINGS AND DETAILS FROM ANOTHER TIME—A WROUGHT-IRON CHANDELIER,
WEIGHTY CURTAINS, A TILED FIREPLACE WITH OVERSIZED ANDIRONS, TACTILE
CUSHIONS, BRICK WALLS—COMBINE TO EVOKE AN ESTABLISHED TROPICAL LOCATION

FREEMANS
WILLIAM TIGERTT
TAAVO SOMER

In the summer of 2004, two friends found a space at the far end of a narrow alley dubbed Freemans, opened a restaurant so named, and created a hit. In the same way that AvroKO's Public introduced one ethos into the contemporary restaurant landscape, Freemans added another: the obsession with taxidermy. A collection that began with just a few pieces expanded along with the restaurant. Two years after it opened, an elaborate installation of Victorian bird boxes—dioramas of fowl—was added over the newly created second bar.

Freemans, an intimate warren of a space with discrete rooms and discreetly connecting hallways, reveals idiosyncratic personal touches bestowed on it by its owners in every twist and turn. Taavo Somer claims to have no idea why his approach has been successful. A profile by David Amsden in *New York Magazine* characterized the restaurateur/ fashion designer—he sells a handmade menswear line at the neighboring Freemans Sporting Club—as a "meticulous imperfectionist." The deliberate but comfortable space is all either a very, very elaborate piece of performance art or utterly honest. The food blends both attitudes. Rustic staples like devils on horseback and macaroni and cheese are artfully presented, bringing a refined version of country cooking to downtown New York City. They are the perfect culinary expression of the reigning interior aesthetic.

With its hidden location, somewhat macabre decoration, beat-up wood tables, and shiny bars, Freemans feels as though it can alter someone's entire personality, to say nothing of mood. Even Somer wasn't immune. When the restaurant first opened, he dove into the character of the space, grooming his hair into a slick 1800s coiffure. The hairstyle may not have remained, but the restaurant's influence on its guests and the New York dining scene will be permanent.

(above)
A FIREPLACE WARMS UP SMALL TABLES; CORRIDORS LEAD TO STILL
MORE HALLWAYS AND SEVERAL SNUG DINING ROOMS THAT COMPRISE THE SPACE

(previous pages)
ORNATE VICTORIAN DIORAMAS DISPLAY A VARIETY OF TAXIDERMIZED BIRDS,
DECORATIONS THAT CONTRAST WITH THE SLIGHTLY GRITTY OVERALL AMBIENCE

(overleaf)
THE TAXIDERMY COLLECTION DISPLAYED IN THE MAIN DINING ROOM

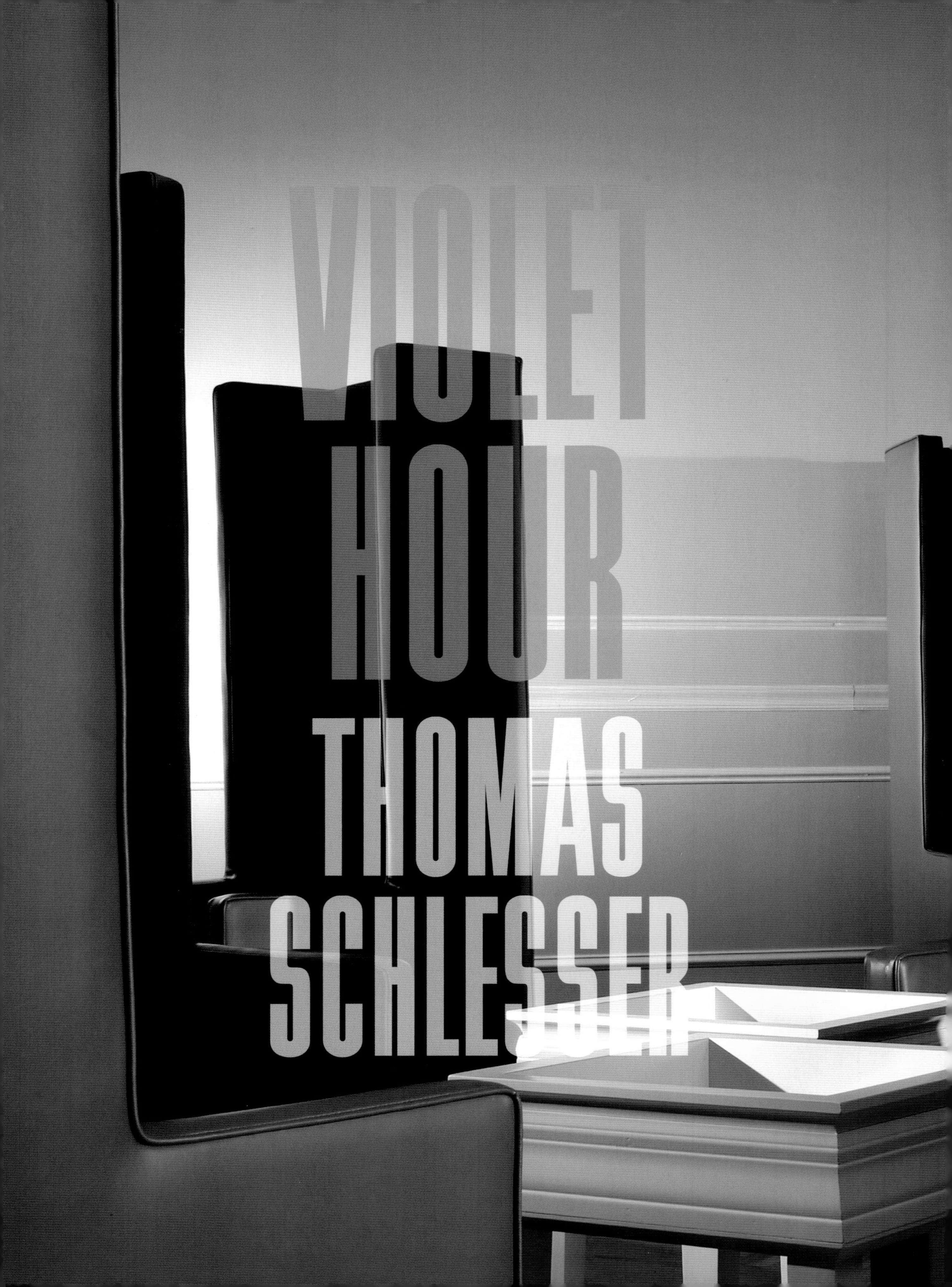
VIOLET
HOUR
THOMAS
SCHLESSER

Its name borrowed from T. S. Eliot's poem *The Waste Land*, its purpose adopted from early-twentieth century bars, and its aesthetic a mix of intimate Georgian and exhibitionist French salon, the Chicago cocktail bar the Violet Hour was designed by New York–based architect Thomas Schlesser to operate on multiple levels, scales, and intimacies.

The search for a contrast between drama and quiet, intensity and relaxation, public and private led Schlesser to segment the large space with a series of heavy curtains, and to then outfit those newly private niches with overscaled furniture that envelops patrons, but through its formidable sizing, also separates them. The main bar itself is similarly divided, turned into a length of segmented smaller bars that are easy to approach and experience.

Schlesser's restaurant and bar design tends towards the contemporary, but the designer found a richness and depth in the "historic dimensional," he says—references he experimented with here. The aesthetic of the cocktails themselves—ingredient-driven, labor-intensive, cooled with ice hand-cracked from one big block—was a profound inspiration, as was the desire to create a space that could encourage playfulness.

The performance starts with the entryway: unmarked, announced only by a single yellow bulb, and hidden in a derelict-looking building. It continues through a corridor that seems part construction site, part *Alice in Wonderland*. Schlesser wanted a disguised entryway to maximize the sense of mystique and discovery, an exclusivity he sees as skipping back in time decades and centuries to the long-standing tradition of the kind of place "you have to know something about to even know there's a place there," he explains. The rawness of the entrance only makes the plushness of the interior that much more evocative and thrilling.

The moments of privacy created and faux-discovered here are part of what make up the feeling of excitement. "This sense of having a little privacy in this public space tends to encourage people to misbehave, to feel like they're on their own, like they can get away with a lot," Schlesser says. "Some of them are in giant overscaled booths, and then some of them are behind curtains." Introducing pockets of intimacy through visual cues like dark materials and smooth, tall-backed chairs is part of what turns this labyrinthine space into a universe of its own seemingly endless potential.

(above left)
HEAVY DRAPERIES DEFINE A HUSHED SENSIBILITY AND SEPARATE SPACES INTO
SMALLER, PRIVATE AREAS

(above right)
SQUARE BARSTOOLS CONTRAST WITH THE FLOWING LINES OF THE DRAPERY WHILE
CONTINUING THE COLOR THEME OF MUTED, DUSKY BLUES

(previous pages)
HIGHLY STYLIZED WING CHAIRS INTRODUCE A PLAY ON SCALE THAT
CONTINUES THROUGHOUT THE BAR

This restaurant and lounge in Paris brings together high fashion, nineties Seattle grunge, and seventeenth-century details. Owned and operated by former Soundgarden frontman Chris Cornell and designed by fashion show producer Alexandre de Betak, Black Calavados is a mix of dark and bright, shiny and matte, ancient history and tomorrow.

De Betak starts every project he creates with a blank black—rather than white—background. "I started with a dark page, and it went all the way to becoming the black lacquered box of the restaurant," the designer says of his approach to the two-story restaurant tucked into a seventeenth-century building in Paris's eighth arrondissement.

When Cornell and de Betak started working on the restaurant, they wanted to be respectful of the venue's original and later history. In its previous incarnation as the Calavados, it was one of Paris's first late-night eating spots, a place where people would go to unwind from a champagne-fueled night by ordering a plate of cassoulet and listening to a soothing piano. De Betak saw both festivity and somberness in the location's past, and sought to reclaim and build upon both.

The tension between celebration and sobriety is everywhere in the restaurant's mutable design. The whiteness of the building's exterior makes that threshold moment of walking up a flight of stairs into the first-floor bar an exercise in contrast, the slip through centuries and aesthetic a jarring removal from contemporary Parisian bustle. The black lacquer was chosen, de Betak says, for its impermanence—it becomes whatever color is shone on it—and for the way it can at once starkly reflect a bright light and warmly absorb a dim one. Maintaining the original venue's integrity meant stripping off many of the later additions like faux ceilings and walls, while keeping the original moldings intact. A step leads to the lounge area, this one in brushed stainless steel surrounded by neon, a brash insertion of modernity in this mixed-reference space.

De Betak wanted a space that acknowledged the darker sides of darkness, but most of all embraced the warmth and intimacy that a shadowy aesthetic can offer. The modernity this designer sought to produce is, as de Betak says, "about our life, today, and the life which used to be there before."

(above)
DRAMATIC LIGHTING CREATES STRONG CONTRASTS IN THE RESTAURANT'S INTERIOR

(previous pages)
BLACK WALLS COME ALIVE AS THEY MIRROR LIGHT FROM STRIPS OF
OVERSIZED BULBS AND REFLECT OTHER COLORS PRESENT IN THE ROOM; THE PLAY OF
SHINY LACQUER AND MATTE GRAY-AND-PURPLE CHAIRS CONTINUES THROUGHOUT
THE SPACE

(above)
A CEILING FRESCO DISCOVERED DURING RENOVATION DATES TO
THE EIGHTEENTH CENTURY

(opposite)
ARCHITECTURAL DETAILS—ORNATE MOLDINGS, A FIREPLACE, A MIRROR OVER
THE MANTEL—ARE PAINTED BLACK TO CREATE A CALMING REFUGE FROM THE BUSY
PARISIAN STREET OUTSIDE

(following pages)
THE BAR INTRODUCES A SENSE OF MOMENTUM AND ENERGY WITH ITS STRONGLY
HORIZONTAL BRIGHT NEON LIGHTING AND METALLIC WALL PANELS

ADOUR
ALAIN DUCASSE
ROCKWELL
GROUP

In early 2007, one of New York City's most expensive and luxurious restaurants—when it first opened, diners were given a choice of twelve possible pens to sign the check with—closed. The eponymous restaurant owned by Alain Ducasse was a leftover agent of a more sumptuous time.

Ducasse, undaunted, swore to return. And in early 2008, in another luxury hotel, this time the St. Regis, Alain Ducasse opened Adour. A David Rockwell design and a new menu emphasizing wine pairings as much as the food itself expressed a shift in direction for the focused Ducasse. It is unabashed, textural, opulent, and its nostalgia lies in an formal decadence, the reprisal of propriety.

The restaurant is also, like many of Rockwell's projects, about myth, storytelling, and narrative. "Design takes the familiar, or what we think is familiar, what triggers cues and memories, and rubs it up against things that are very new," Rockwell says. The storied St. Regis Hotel provides the familiarity—the city retains a collective memory of exquisite meals in this former Lespinasse space. "Nothing in the St. Regis is truly original," Rockwell points out. "The old is romanticized."

The designers took this stately past and slammed it up against a hypercontemporary, high-technology take on wine culture, buttressed with an aesthetic clarity that bridges the gap between then and now. A backlit glass wall molded to the shape of the central dining room's original architecture defines this approach. The light melting through this thin veil calls out in sharp relief an etched grapevine pattern by artist Casey Maher in a perfect confluence of traditional motif and modern reinterpretation. Rockwell was inspired by rituals—from the thrill of the first grape crush through a swirl of decanting to the particular oenophile language—and that sense of purposeful enjoyment, with delineated and outlined ways to be entertained, crops up throughout the space.

A goatskin bar highlights Adour's biggest technological achievement—touch-screen capabilities projected onto textile. But it is the spray of simple, bubble-like lights that illuminates it that speaks to the sheer pleasure that comes with the acknowledgment of this kind of privilege and the champagne it so often involves. Created out of gold-flecked glass by the artist Ken Gangbar, the hanging detail reinforces the luxury of the atmosphere while providing a nod to Ducasse's new playful attitude. "The bubbles," Rockwell says, "came up as a way to create a wall that was a memory of a wall."

(above)
DINING ROOMS INCLUDE SUBTLE REFERENCES TO WINE—UPHOLSTERY
IN DEEP REDS AND GOLDEN YELLOWS AND ART WITH FLOWING, SWIRLING MOTIFS

(previous pages)
A WALL OF CHAMPAGNE BUBBLE–LIKE GLASS BALLS CREATED BY ARTIST
KEN GANGBAR FLOAT BEHIND A GOATSKIN BAR

(overleaf)
AN ABSTRACTED, ETCHED GRAPEVINE PATTERN COVERS THE WALLS;
PLUSH CARPETING AND CHAIRS ADD TEXTURE AND LUXURY TO THE SPACE

ALLEN &
DELANCEY

JASON VOLENEC

RKIT DESIGN

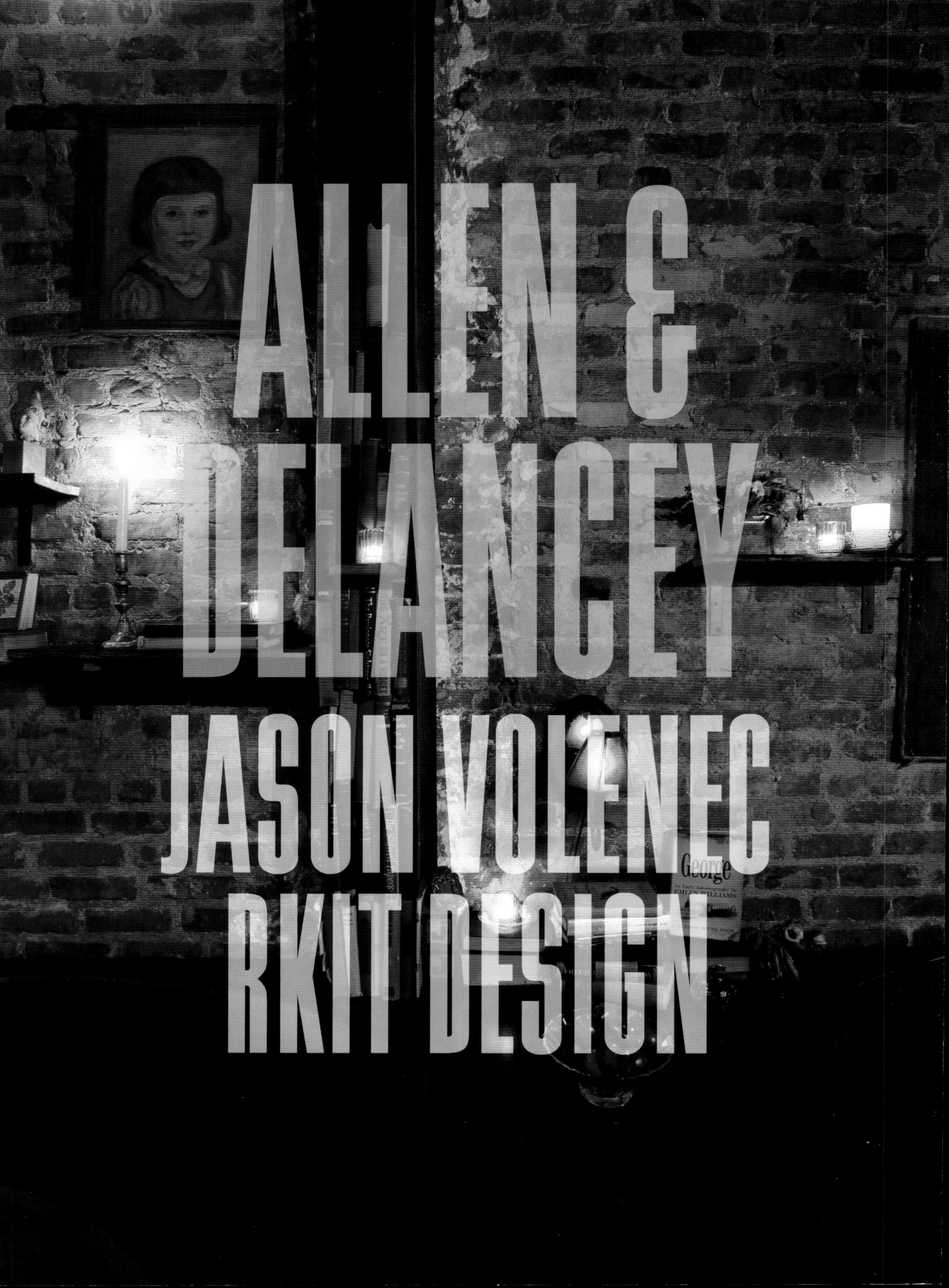

Two years after Adolf Loos, radical Austrian architect and author of the seminal essay "Ornament and Crime," designed the American Bar in Vienna, a narrow brick building went up on the corner of Allen and Delancey Streets on New York's Lower East Side. Then, the area was a crowded immigrant landing ground; now it is a mix of new money and old style, contemporary and historic architecture, and layered interiors.

Architect Jason Volenec borrowed from Loos for his design of the restaurant occupying that building since 2007, Allen & Delancey. Volenec imagined this "creative immigrant" arriving in 1909 and assessing the site. "It's almost as if he designed the original proportions of the space, and then over the years many different people came through and left their marks, creating layers and layers of history and different stories," the designer says. "It doesn't represent one history or one historical style. By an amalgam of history, it becomes contemporary." A three-part layout—entrance bar, central dining room, and back cavern—gives the space a sense of forward momentum, of travel through (nonlinear) history. Velvet curtains split the central dining space and offer a textural respite from the exposed brick walls. The black mirror bar—a nod to Loos's aesthetic decrying unnecessary ornamentation in favor of purer, truthful decoration—in the slender front area was directly inspired by the narrowness of the American Bar, as were the more abstracted and geometric shapes in the restaurant's detailing, such as the careful repetition of votive candles and mix of horizontal and vertical bookshelves.

As much as these disparate decorative elements evoke the past, so too did the menu crafted for the restaurant's launch and first year. Developed by Neil Ferguson—a soft-spoken Englishman, a layering of history that itself only too perfectly and practically articulates Volenec's design approach—the food perfectly complemented the historical entrenchment of the restaurant's aesthetic. A dish called "Cabbage, Beef, and Onion" shared menu space with an old-fashioned côte du boeuf for two, and caramelized bone marrow arrived, for extra decadence, with caviar.

(above left)
THE FRONT DINING ROOM INTRODUCES THE USE OF EXPOSED BRICK AND THE
ECLECTIC MIX OF OBJECTS AND ART THAT CHARACTERIZE THE RESTAURANT'S DESIGN

(above right)
A SPARE CHANDELIER ALLOWS CANDLES AND SMALL LAMPS TO ILLUMINATE
BOOKSHELVES AND OBJECTS AT EYE LEVEL

(overleaf left)
A LONG BLACK BAR REFERENCES THE ORIGINAL INSPIRATION FOR THE SPACE,
ADOLF LOOS'S 1907 AMERICAN BAR IN VIENNA

(overleaf right)
A VIEW FROM THE ENTRY THROUGH THE RESTAURANT REVEALS HEAVY
RED STAGE-STYLE CURTAINS THAT DIVIDE THE SPACE

MONTAUK HOUSE

ROBIN STANDEFER
STEPHEN ALESCH

The owners of this home on Long Island's east end never stop working. Founders of design firm Roman and Williams, the couple uses both their city loft and this larger domestic space in Montauk as a laboratory to continue the evolution of their own memory- and narrative-driven design.

The pair purchased this open beach house because of its loftlike plan and their desire to have a home close to nature. "Other properties we looked at had all these dividing walls, and Robin and I would both just get claustrophobic," Alesch says of their immediate pull towards this 2,500-square-foot space that encompasses a kitchen, living room, and dining room. The couple added a studio to dedicate space to the exploration of creative urges. The two are nearly always within earshot and eyesight, and Montauk's single-block layout is ideal for their life in tandem.

It's that cutting of a channel between two things—history and today, weight and light, gravity and articulation—that extends through all the cues of the couple's design work. Examples are everywhere in this weekend house: each object is introduced with such a sense of depth and purpose that the place transcends trend. Furnishings and decorative objects are from mixed periods; the overall scheme is not intended to be easily navigated, but to provoke thought and cause the eye to linger over individual elements.

Direction begins in the central kitchen—Alesch believes that a stove in a true home is never cold—and continues through the living area complete with a taxidermized black bird and a whale bone. "I use references like bones, eggshells, and parchment paper," Standefer explains, "to create a lived-in and nature-infused space that resonates throughout the immediate site and out into the world." This is about Roman and Williams's ethos, their aesthetic, and their life. This house on Montauk is the microcosm of their world.

(above)
GROUPS OF CURIOUS HISTORIC OBJECTS—INCLUDING A HIPPOPOTAMUS SKULL—SERVE
AS INSPIRATION IN A STUDIO FURNISHED WITH AN ECLECTIC MIX OF ANTIQUES

(previous pages)
A BRIGHTLY LIT KITCHEN REMAINS HISTORICALLY ROOTED WITH AN ORNATE
TEA KETTLE, THIN CANDLES, AND A COPIOUS USE OF TRADITIONAL MATERIALS LIKE
WOOD, BRICK, LEATHER, AND GALVANIZED STEEL

(above)
TAXIDERMIZED ANIMALS ADD INTEREST TO A ROOM THAT USES WOODS, FURS, AND
METAL TO CREATE LAYERS OF TEXTURE

(opposite)
A CURVED PIECE OF WHALE SKELETON ECHOES THE SHAPE OF A HANDMADE
LAMP AND CONTRASTS WITH THE STRAIGHT LINES OF ITS SUPPORTING TABLE AND
NEARBY ARMCHAIR

(above)
A BLACK-FRAMED WINDOW, DARK FLOWER PRINT, AND FURS INJECT AN
OTHERWISE BRIGHT ROOM WITH DARK, HISTORIC ACCENTS

(opposite)
CORAL, A SPINY FISH, AND A SEASHELL-ENCRUSTED MIRROR LEND AN UNDERSEA
THEME TO THIS GUEST BEDROOM

(overleaf)
A WALL OF IDYLLIC OCEAN-RELATED SCENES THAT REFERENCES ALESCH'S LOVE OF
SURFING KEEPS COMPANY WITH A COLLECTION OF ANTIQUE NAUTICAL INSTRUMENTS,
A GNARLED WOOD LAMP, AND AN ASSORTMENT OF SHELLS IN THE STUDIO

CLIFT
HOTEL
PHILIPPE STARCK

When Ian Schrager decided to renovate this iconic hotel with Philippe Starck as the design lead, it came as little surprise that many San Franciscans were anxious about the change. The Clift, long a beloved city institution, was prized for its reassuring familiarity as much as its luxury.

The focus of skepticism about any renovation was the Redwood Room, built in 1934 in the reigning Art Deco style. As legend has it, its enormous bar was carved from the wood of a single tree. It was the kind of place that immediately sparked memories of a first-date drink or a meaningful family moment, so it was exactly the kind of place that people organized to fight to keep. But with Starck's guidance, it turned out to be the kind of place that could survive a renovation with the core of its history intact.

In 2001 the playful designer, riffing off the past and its relationship to today, retained the room's paneling crafted from 2,000-year-old redwood but added an etched glass top to the original bar, and replaced the 1970s Gustav Klimt prints with plasma monitors that cycle through digital palimpsests of the originals—cheeky interpretations of the original Art Deco space. It became a hot spot in the way all Schrager's properties seem magically to do, and the press about the reopening focused on how remarkably satisfied those who had wanted to protect it were with what the Morgans Hotel Group had created.

It helped that it was fun. The gray-plastered lobby is punched up with the introduction of an 18-foot-high bronze fireplace and Starck's playful gigantic version of a chair. The off-lobby Living Room is also given a touch of whimsy with a grid of black-and-white photographs of toys. The history of the Clift's renovation reflects most typical reactions to the new—a knee-jerk preservationist instinct kicks in, a cry rings out for the retention of a memory-saturated place, followed eventually, tentatively by an acceptance that while times change and details shift form, the result can sometimes be a comfortable evolution rather than a rash obliteration.

(above)
MISMATCHED FURNISHINGS AND AN OVERSCALED LOUIS XV CHAIR POP AGAINST
THE LOBBY'S COOL GRAY WALLS

(previous pages)
A STYLIZED FAUX-REPRODUCTION CHAISE, COYLY ANGULAR LAMP, AND
PHOTOGRAPHS OF PLASTIC TOYS BY ARTIST JEAN-BAPTISTE MONDINO INTRODUCE
WHIMSY IN THE LIVING ROOM

(overleaf)
THE ICONIC REDWOOD ROOM'S ORIGINAL ART DECO DETAILING BLENDS
HARMONIOUSLY WITH ELEMENTS INTRODUCED DURING STARCK'S RENOVATION,
INCLUDING THE EXTENSIVE ETCHED-GLASS BAR

A DRAPED WALL PROVIDES GEOMETRIC CONTRAST TO SINUOUS PEDESTAL TABLES;
CANDLELIGHT IS REFLECTED IN THE SPACE'S MANY MIRRORED SURFACES

(above)
CHANDELIERS DRIPPING CRYSTALS AND LAMPS THAT CHEEKILY REINTERPRET
THEIR FORM ILLUMINATE A SUITE

(overleaf left)
TEXTURED SURFACES ATTRACT ATTENTION IN THE MAIN LOBBY; THE RECEPTION DESK
IS CARVED FROM A SINGLE PIECE OF MAHOGANY, AND THE 18-FOOT-HIGH BRONZE
FIREPLACE IS BY FRENCH ARTIST GÉRARD GAROUSTE

(overleaf right)
WEIGHTY DRAPERY AND ETCHED-GLASS TABLES IN THE ASIA DE CUBA RESTAURANT
ECHO THE DÉCOR OF THE ADJACENT REDWOOD ROOM

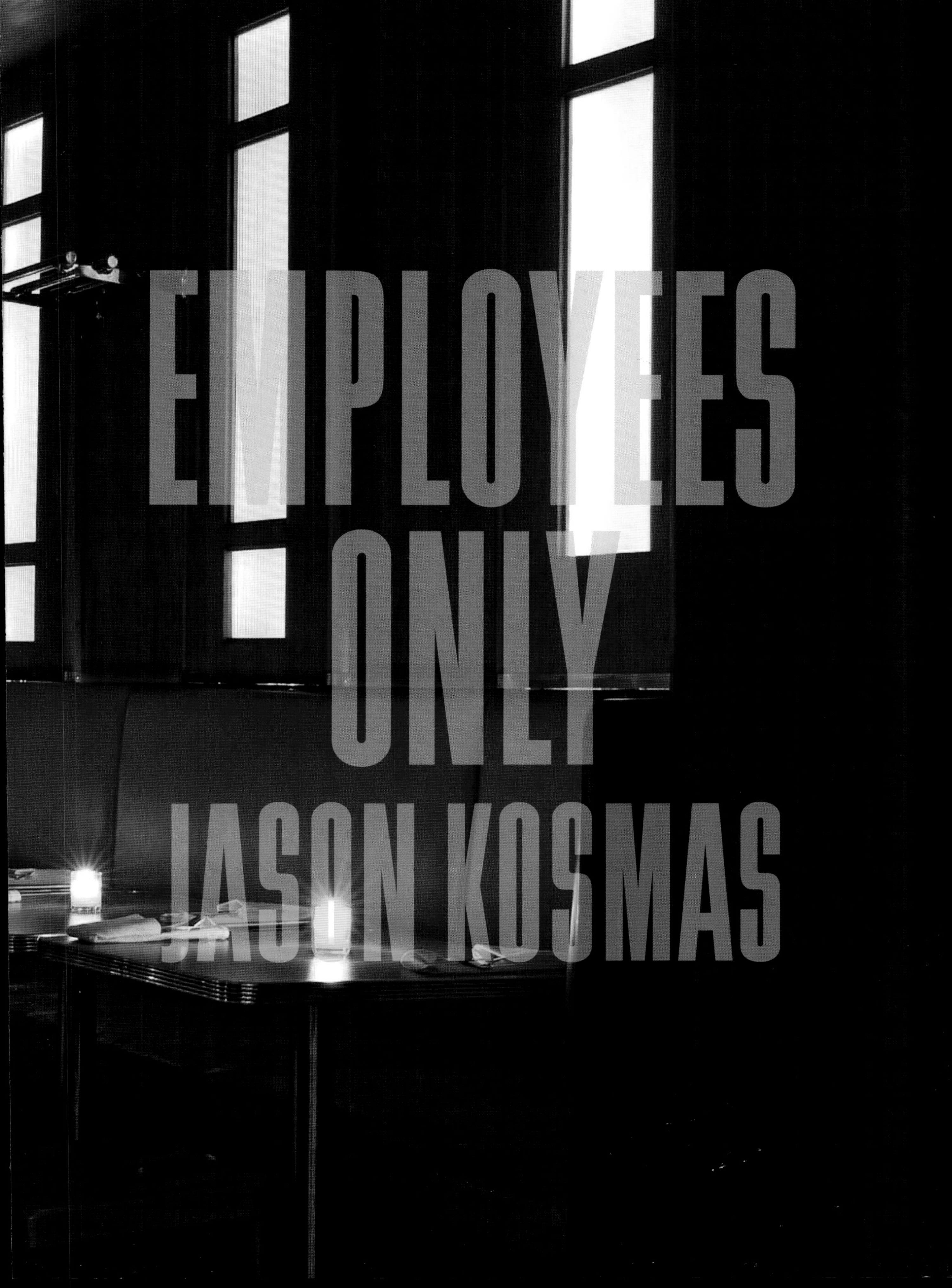
EMPLOYEES
ONLY
JASON KOSMAS

Inspired by Prohibition, invented with a backstory, and armed with an impressive cocktail menu informed by period tastes, Employees Only opened in Manhattan's West Village in 2005. Designed to be an updated version of a speakeasy, the cooks and bartenders corrected long-established classic dishes and drinks for a contemporary palate, and reinterpreted an Art Deco interior to keep the seductive appeal of an illicit institution.

"We didn't want it to be like a movie set," owner Jason Kosmas says. "But we wanted it to have the feel of something that had been around, that you might have stumbled upon." The design was top-down, soup-to-nuts, and encompassed everything from the menu—hand-cut tableside-prepared steak tartare, elderflower cocktails, smoked trout— to the shape of the bar, curved so that everyone can see everyone else.

From a tarot-card-reader-occupied vestibule behind a sign with such subtle lettering that it could easily be overlooked, through the central bar area detailed with mahogany paneling, red-painted walls, and worn-leather barstools, and up to the main dining space that is part ocean liner, part Parisian lounge, the designer incorporated fantastical details that set the mood. Visually, he articulates the tension between the familiar routine inherent in daily life and the thrill of possibility. "People go out because they want something to happen to them that's different than their normal lives," Kosmas says. "The idea behind the speakeasy is that, without doing anything wrong, you create this illusion of naughtiness."

It is naughtiness—late night, champagne and oysters, who knows what could happen—but tempered with a propriety that comes through in the smaller design details: softly illuminated artwork, dressed-up waiters, that tableside service. Employees Only took the vulgarity of original speakeasies and infused it with twenty-first century savvy. It gives people a chance to travel through time, to have a peek at how much more freeing outlets were in a society that was much more strict. Employees Only gives license to flirt, so long as you sit up straight while you do it, and reason to indulge, since when would you ever smoke your own trout? It rewrites history, re-creates the past, and in doing so, defines the present.

(above left)
ART DECO DETAILS—THE FIREPLACE SCREEN, MAHOGANY-PANELED WALLS,
AND RECESSED CEILING—EVOKE THE PROHIBITION ERA

(above right)
GLOWING SHELVES LINE THE WALL BEHIND THE CURVED BRASS AND BLACK
LACQUER BAR

(previous pages)
A CURVED WALL INSET WITH A SERIES OF VERTICAL LIGHT PANELS,
LEATHER BANQUETTES, BRIGHT RED TABLES, AND PERIOD DECORATIONS COMBINE
TO ESTABLISH A WARM, VINTAGE FEEL IN THE MAIN DINING SPACE

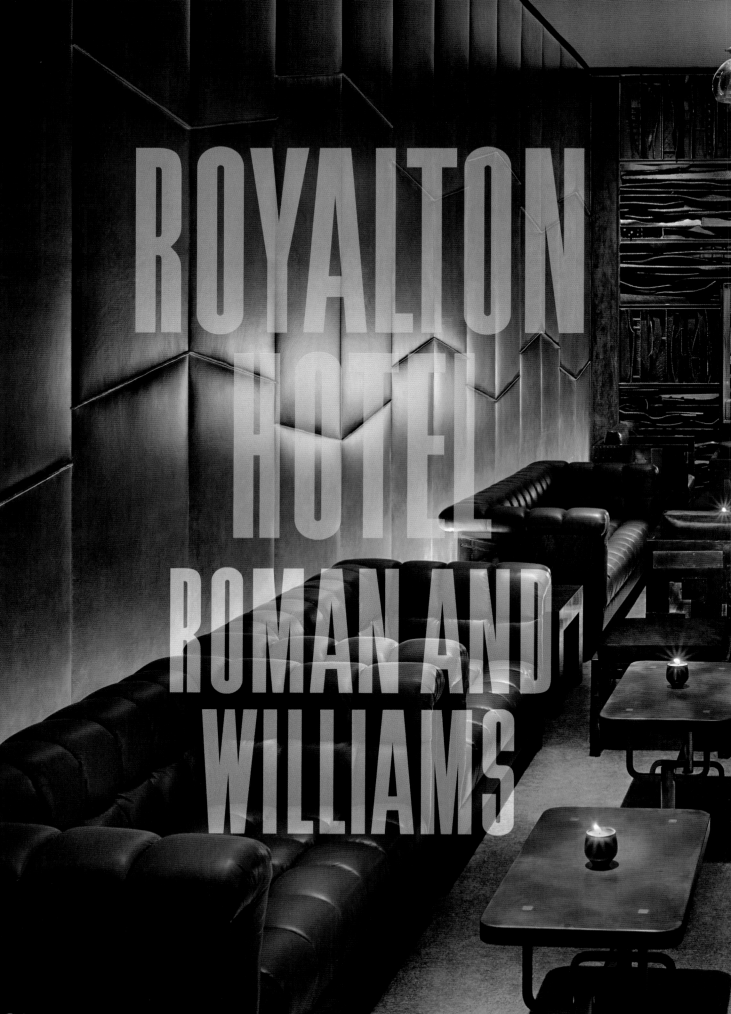

ROYALTON
HOTEL
ROMAN AND
WILLIAMS

It was much nostalgia about nostalgia when this renovation of Philippe Starck's iconic Royalton Hotel lobby was unveiled at the end of 2007. Out with theatrical pop, Roman and Williams said through their design. In with warmth and comfort.

The space itself is difficult: a block-length lobby, narrow as it is low-ceilinged, with dropped pockets that could only be filled with rows of seating to one side, a cut-out bar area to the other, and a restaurant to the back. Roman and Williams focused on what patrons seek in a cosmopolitan hotel lobby—the potential for easy anonymity, the desire for solitary comfort, the possibility of very quick friend-making—in reshaping this daunting expanse.

The famous catwalk effect remains, but now inviting sunken cocoons filled with decadently comfortable furniture give visitors the option of being snugly hidden, rather than constantly on display, if they so choose. Clubbiness and a sense of heightened luxury still pervade, though today in a more subtle atmosphere. Details—like a salvaged, dark-metal screen that runs along a third of the lobby's wall, handmade bronze side tables, and chairs and sofas draped with furs—combine to create a mood that is gritty and rough.

Power breakfast restaurant Brasserie 44 of the late nineties and early aughts, when the media still power breakfasted, has been reinvented, too. Rounded forms are used to encourage holistic connections through-out the space. Arching webs of rope that separate rounded banquette from rounded banquette, brightly luminescent globe lamps, and a mix of smoothly polished exotic woods create a nautical environment.

When this interior was opened to the public, there was revolt. Critics decried the updated design. A landmark had been destroyed, they said. Philippe Starck was irreplaceable, an icon for the age. It was true, had been true, but what Roman and Williams created was a new icon for a new age. This hotel lobby is no longer for supermodels and the people who hope to meet them, for editors who run glamorous magazines, or for the hungry writers they hire. It is a break for everyone from the everyday, a second of respite from the constant striving. This Royalton is about a sophisticated kind of fun: one that involves intimacy and truth.

(above)
THE BLOCK-LENGTH, NARROW LOBBY HALL IS VISUALLY BROKEN INTO A SERIES
OF SMALLER SPACES BY A VINTAGE VENINI CHANDELIER AND A SERIES OF CLOSELY
PLACED COLUMNS

(previous pages)
TACTILITY REIGNS IN THE LOBBY: RICH VELVET AND LEATHER UPHOLSTERY CONTRASTS
WITH TEXTURED BRONZE ON THE SIDES OF ARMCHAIRS AND SOFAS; EACH WALL
SURFACE FEATURES A DIFFERENT PATTERN—ABSTRACTED HERRINGBONE TO THE LEFT,
INTRICATE HAND-FORGED CAST BRONZE AROUND THE FIREPLACE, AND A STRINGED
SCREEN OF EXOTIC WOODS ON THE RIGHT

(overleaf)
SLENDER WOOD PANELS AND BRONZE DETAILS IN NOOK OF A BAR NEAR THE HOTEL'S
ENTRANCE CONTINUE THE SAME DARK AESTHETIC FOUND THROUGHOUT THE LOBBY

(above)
CURVED BANQUETTES, ROPE WEBBING, AND HANGING GLOBE LIGHTS CONTRIBUTE
TO A WARM, NAUTICAL FEEL IN RESTAURANT BRASSERIE 44

(opposite)
THE CRISP LINES OF OVERSIZED CUSHIONS, CHAIRS COVERED IN SOUTH AFRICAN
SPRINGBOK, AND AN ARTICULATED SCREEN IN THE REAR OF THE LOBBY
CREATE A TEXTURAL AND EXPERIENTIAL SEPARATION FROM THE MORE DECADENT FORMS
FOUND NEAR THE FRONT

(overleaf)
A GRATE SALVAGED FROM A BUILDING FACADE IN FRANCE BECOMES A WALL SCREEN IN
A DROPPED SEATING AREA; SQUARE, HARD-EDGED CHAIRS BRUSH UP AGAINST
OVERSTUFFED LEATHER SOFAS IN A MIX OF MATERIALS THAT REITERATES THE TENSION
BETWEEN SMOOTHNESS AND TEXTURE IN EVIDENCE THROUGHOUT THE SPACE

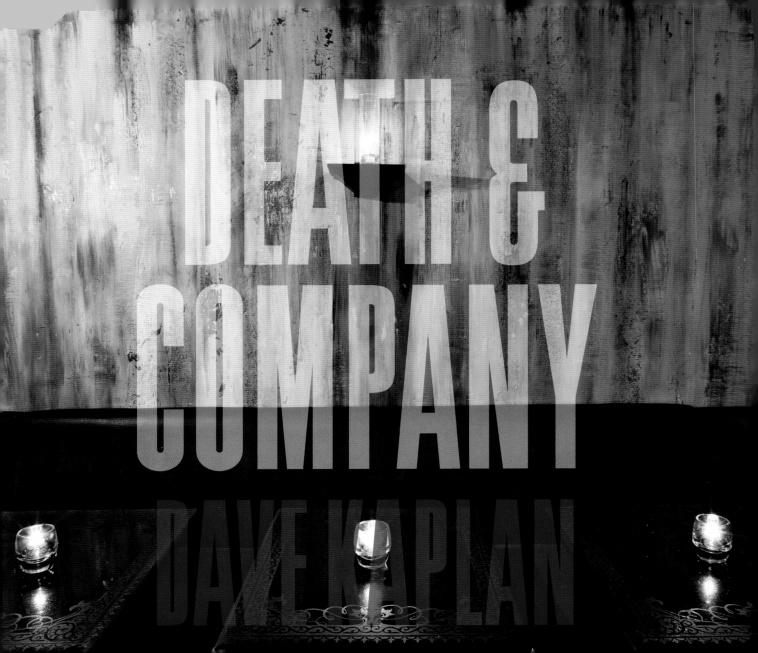

When Dave Kaplan decided to open a bar with his brother Ravi in New York's East Village, the twenty-four-year-old first-time restaurateur decided he might as well, along with learning how to run a bar, figure out how to design the place himself.

Kaplan trained for the hospitality business with a short-lived career as a Las Vegas VIP host, for the aesthetic side of things with a degree in fine arts that focused on photography, and for the social side with a minor in sociology. Mostly, though, Kaplan prepared himself by thinking about the kinds of environments that struck him as honest, and set about embodying that quality. The photography background influenced Death & Company's looks, and the sociology interest helped Kaplan create its mood.

The carefully crafted visual identity starts with the exterior. Three wood-beam panels suddenly pop out against the typical East Village tenement-and-bar streetscape, each spotlit from above. The central panel—what turns out to be the door—has a brighter and larger spotlight, shining onto an inlaid steel piece that reads, in elaborate script, "Death & Co."

"I'm interested in the idea of new permanence," Kaplan says. "I wanted a place that, whether it's new or five years old, feels like it has been there forever." Kaplan acknowledges that Death & Company finds its place in a lineage of similarly themed spaces, and that he was inspired by existing establishments with a like-minded dedication to real immutability, expressed through tactility.

He cites the 1919 Volstead Act and the swift end it brought to nightlife when speaking about his own contribution to current after-hours social activity. He views today's revelry as a continuing celebration of the end of Prohibition. It isn't a literal adoption, though, as much as a romanticized idea. Death & Company is a bar that operates in homage to its explicit set of referents, and articulates the freedom that comes with commitment, the particular clarity that distilling a set of cues and histories down to its most idealized state can bring.

(above)
MOMENTUM IS CONVEYED IN THE NARROW SPACE BY A LONG, PANELED CEILING;
A TEXTURED WALL OF LIGHT WOOD INTRODUCES A WORN AND WEATHERED ELEMENT
TO A ROOM OF OTHERWISE HIGHLY POLISHED SURFACES

(previous page left)
TABLES ARE LASER-ETCHED WITH AN INTRICATE DESIGN BY A TATTOO ARTIST

(previous page right)
A CARVED DOOR HANDLE IN A PURPOSELY VAGUE FIGURATIVE SHAPE AND THE
INSET SCRIPT PROVIDE CLUES TO THE INTERIOR'S DESIGN

When the first Ace Hotel—named with a nod to the simultaneous high-low nature of that particular playing card—opened in 1999 in Seattle, it provided a more-minimalist-than-minimalist response to the latent slickness of the time. Owner Alex Calderwood fashioned the hotel from an existing structure, embracing its tiny rooms, shared bathrooms, and insane asylum layout, and turning what could have been seen as architectural defects into experiential upsides.

In 2007, the Ace came to Portland. The setting and times were different, and Calderwood chose to keep things specific, even local. "Beyond creating a sense of memory—which for us comes a lot from instinct," he says, "we try to engender a sense of place." The Oregon city prizes its serious music scene, magnificent landscape, and extremely progressive urbanism and environmentalism. Translating that indie, nature-loving culture into immediate physical indicators of place for the lobby entrance meant bins of vinyl records leaning against vintage trunks, and an ornate (if well-used) sofa buttressed by a roughly-sawn log for a side table. Local artists contributed murals throughout the hotel, ranging from a tattoolike wall sketch to a hyperrealist depiction of a cat.

Deeper historical references come in the form of claw-foot tubs, produced in 1912—the same year the hotel building was first constructed—and in the use of Douglas fir salvaged from the bones of the original structure, now turned into desks and counters. The rooms' bedside tables were made from beams taken from a garage just across the street from the Ace, the lobby's coffee table from a reclaimed industrial fire door.

Purpose and use shift with the transformation of materials from one home and identity to another, and this hotel is an example of how slow and careful adaptation can combine to create a sense of permanence.

(above left)
A WOODEN CARD FILE AND ROUND STOOLS ADD PERSONALITY TO THE MEZZANINE
BUSINESS LOUNGE

(above right)
DARK CURTAINS AND A REFURBISHED CLAW-FOOT BATHTUB WITH A BLACK EXTERIOR
ARE SURPRISINGLY MODERN TOUCHES IN A HISTORICALLY INFORMED BATHROOM

(previous pages)
THE MURAL *LARRY* BY LOCAL ARTIST BRENT WICK GRACES A GUEST ROOM;
A VINYL TURNTABLE NEXT TO THE REUPHOLSTERED SOFA INTRODUCES PERIOD
ELEMENTS TO THE MODERN HOTEL

(above)
A MURAL REFERENCING MUSIC AND VINYL RECORDS, BY KENZO MINAMI, POPS
AGAINST DARK PEWTER PAINT IN THIS GUEST ROOM

(opposite)
RECLAIMED WOOD LINES THE BACK WALL OF A GUEST ROOM WHILE TWO
INDUSTRIAL LAMPS BRIGHTEN ITS HUNTER-CHIC AESTHETIC

(overleaf left)
A JORG AND OLIF COMMUTER BICYCLE LEANS AGAINST THE DARK WOOD
PANELING OF THE BOOK-LINED LOBBY

(overleaf right)
COUCHES SURROUND A TABLE CREATED FROM SALVAGED MATERIALS; A FOUND
HOTEL SIGN IS A LITERAL EXAMPLE OF ADOPTION AND TRANSFORMATION

DOUBLE
CROWN
AVROKO

For its second owned-and-operated New York City restaurant, the team of architects at AvroKO cultivated what they refer to as an Indo-Chinese-Colonial look. The design of both the restaurant and its accompanying bar, Madame Geneva, was inspired by idealized interpretations of British involvement in the East, and chef Brad Farmerie developed an Asian-inflected multinational menu to complete the theme.

"We talked a lot about warm weather climate, about a kind of commonwealth idea, about military and sporting," principal Kristina O'Neal says. The name Double Crown was chosen for its evocation of two regal identities—Britain and its Colonial Empire. It also introduces the concept of connectivity suggested throughout the space. The entryway opens onto two long wooden tables that mirror the dimensions of the bar. This space is lit by dropped lanterns that are themselves reflected in a mirror, and add points of light against the backdrop of an exposed brick wall. Toward the rear, an archway leads to a second dining area detailed with white, paneled walls that evoke the refined mood of a private British club.

AvroKO's tongue-in-cheek approach to reference is effective at making spaces with many layers of meaning accessible. "Double Crown is playful. We used historical and hand-carved pieces," O'Neal explains. "But in an ultra-hyper-realized way that layers real things from a temple in Asia or India with neon idols." The restaurant offers a little bit of a flash on history, brightness on darkness, emotion on architecture.

The heavy teak wood that forms the boxy coffered ceiling and is used throughout the structure lends weight and is a recognizably tropical material. Choosing to building the restaurant into the bones of an existing building in the heart of a historic neighborhood allowed for just enough of a sense of fantasy—some imported from Asia, some from the architects' imaginations—to make a temporary suspension of disbelief about actual location easy, and render this newly created world exciting.

(above)
A CURVED CORNER BANQUETTE IN THE RESTAURANT'S ATTACHED BAR, MADAME
GENEVA, OFFERS PRIVACY AND A SIMPLIFIED VERSION OF MOTIFS USED ELSEWHERE
IN THE RESTAURANT

(previous pages)
EXPOSED BRICK, A WALL PANELED IN A MIX OF FLORAL PRINTS PAINTED BLUE,
RED CLUB CHAIRS, AND REPURPOSED ELEVATOR GATES CREATE AN UNDERGROUND
ATMOSPHERE THAT IS PART DUNGEON AND PART FANTASY

(above)
NEON INTRODUCES AN ELEMENT OF WHIMSY AND FUTURISM TO THE LARGELY
BACKWARDS-LOOKING DESIGN

(opposite)
WOVEN CHAIRS—AT ONCE PROPER AND WARMLY TACTILE—AND LAMPS CREATED
FROM REPURPOSED FAN BELTS HANG FROM A BOXY COFFERED CEILING

(above)
HEAVY CHAINS SUSPENDED FROM THE CEILING BETWEEN DINING ROOMS ARE
DELIBERATELY HUNG WHERE VISITORS WILL HAVE TO WALK AROUND THEM, FORCING
CONTEMPLATION OF THE INTRICATE FORMS

(opposite)
INTRICATELY CARVED WALLS ADD TACTILITY TO A DOWNSTAIRS HALL

(overleaf)
WHITE-PANELED WALLS BRIGHTEN THE MAIN DINING ROOM WHILE ENDOWING IT WITH
A SENSE OF HISTORY; VOTIVES ARE SUSPENDED FROM PERIOD COAT HOOKS

BOURBON &
BRANCH
FUTUREBARS

There are moments in which it seems as though the universe is communicating through a series of signs. Brian Sheehy's discovery of a virtually intact 1920s speakeasy in the basement of the speakeasy-style bar he was planning to open in San Francisco's rough-and-rumble Tenderloin District was just one of those moments.

Sheehy and his partners Dahi Donnelly and Doug Dalton—inspired by the success of a few Roaring Twenties–theme parties they had thrown at their existing bar, Swig—spent six months looking for a place to open a speakeasy. They found one half a block away (sign one), were able to convince the owner to sell after six months of pleading (sign two), and finally gained access to the basement despite the fact that the owner had, in a fit of basement-fearing superstition, thrown away the key (sign three). "We cut through the hinges on the trapdoor and there it was, in all its glory from the 1920s," Sheehy says. Other design inspirations came from geographically further afield, including visits to New York and Chicago, and hours of library research during which the partners pored through hundreds of glamorous pictures of actual speakeasies.

Sheehy wanted to make sure that the forbidden-practice appeal would stick, so he delved into speakeasy lore and imposed a series of social restrictions that enhance the theme. Passwords are needed for access, required reservations are given for set durations of time only, and no standing is allowed at the bar—patrons must be properly seated. The owners also developed an electronic reservation manage-ment program, but hid everything technological, like the point-of-sale system and the touch screens, under the bar, favoring a zingy antique cash register instead.

Since opening in 2006, Sheehy has added two spaces to increase capacity—a library, which does allow standing, and Russell's Room, named in honor of the cigar shop that occupied Bourbon & Branch's location during the actual Prohibition years, but operated as so much more. "When people first come in, they feel like they're transported back in time," Sheehy says. "But then they'll notice that some of the shapes have a modern touch in them." The entire aesthetic of the space creates a continuity between historical speakeasies and the Bourbon & Branch team's interpretation of them. This bar pushes that purposeful secrecy forward, for a new generation.

(above)
AN ART DECO-INFLUENCED CHANDELIER BY LOCAL ARTIST IVAN MORA
ILLUMINATES THE BAR; ITS SHARP TENTACLES DRAW THE EYE UP FROM THE GLOWING
BAR AND TOWARD THE PRESSED TIN CEILING

(previous pages)
EXPOSED BRICK BEHIND THE BAR READS AS A SECOND PATTERN WHEN
JUXTAPOSED WITH DEEP RED WALLPAPER; METAL BARSTOOLS ANCHORED TO THE
FLOOR CREATE A REGULATED ENVIRONMENT

IN THE J. J. RUSSELL CIGAR ROOM—NAMED FOR THE SHOP THAT ORIGINALLY
OCCUPIED THE SPACE—A BLACK CHANDELIER, RED VELVET COUCHES, AND TUFTED
LEATHER PANELING REITERATE THE SITE'S HISTORY

A TRUE SPEAKEASY FEELING PERVADES THE LIBRARY SPACE, WHICH REQUIRES A
DIFFERENT PASSWORD FOR ENTRY THAN THE REST OF THE BAR

NOHO LOFT
ROBIN STANDEFER
STEPHEN ALESCH

When founding partners of the firm Roman and Williams, Robin Standefer and Stephen Alesch, relocated from Los Angeles to an apartment in New York City's NoHo district, they brought their artistic sensibility, tested on the sets of the movies *Addicted to Love* and *Zoolander*, with them. Their loft is the very heart of their creative world, the laboratory in which they hone their interior design skills by moving a graphite object three inches to the left, an apothecary jar two feet to the right, just to see how it feels—and, more importantly—operates. The space is visual evidence of their approach to life: making-above-all and creativity-no-matter-what.

The apartment, punctuated by a living room on one brightly lit end and a bedroom and a library on the other, is full of objects artfully arrayed to catch the eye and provoke thought. The mood is heavy, weighty, serious. "Irony and humor in design don't appeal to us," Standefer says. Neither does following current trends. "I think that there's an industrial trend and a historical trend, which Stephen and I don't feel we fit into."

For all its attention to minute detail and its carefully edited selection of pieces, the space feels completely honest, like a legitimate living space rather than a de facto design gallery. Alesch describes his aversion to choosing items on the basis of looks or theme alone through the example of an earlier house the pair helped design. "The owners bought all this farm equipment, guns, taxidermy, and cowboy boots and lined them up in the hallway. I thought it was horrific—I hated to see those boots unused, planted there." He saw it as a "nostalgic kind of catering." And so, every single object in their house—from a tiny camera obscura to a salvaged file cabinet—is either in use or potentially useful.

For Standefer and Alesch, layering historical references on top of each other is part of the heavy narrative that their architecture produces. For Standefer, owning a piece of taxidermy isn't about fitting into a stylistic sensibility, but rather a way of commemorating a life and sustaining it forward so that the space it's displayed in inspires memory. This can be both micro- and macrocontextual, operating on the level of personal as well as cultural collective memory. The focus on memory doesn't mean that their work or their apartment is about living in the past—the emotion that Roman and Williams projects produce by layering multiple historical referents and moments transcends an easy visual translation, and is a completely modern and contemporary experience.

(top)
DRIED FLOWERS WITH SCULPTURAL FORMS AND GLASS JARS FILLED
WITH BRIGHT INGREDIENTS ADD LEVITY TO A POCKET OF KITCHEN SPACE

(above)
ROBIN STANDEFER'S DESK IS COVERED WITH OBJECTS THAT INSPIRE HER,
SUCH AS ANTIQUE INKWELLS AND A SCULPTURE OF A HAND

(previous pages)
A CONSTANTLY CHANGING ARRANGEMENT OF APOTHECARY BOTTLES,
DRIED CORAL, DRAWING MATERIALS, AND FRAMED PRINTS RESTS ON A
SALVAGED CHALKBOARD AND FILING CABINET

(overleaf)
BOOKSHELVES AND ANTIQUE CABINETS FIND A PLACE IN THIS LONG,
STRAIGHTFORWARD SPACE UNIFIED BY A GLOSSY BLACK FLOOR; A SURFBOARD—
ALESCH IS OBSESSED—RESTS BENEATH A VINTAGE TABLE

BROWN TONES, WOODS, AND A BEARSKIN THROW ADD SOFTNESS TO A LIVING
ROOM FILLED WITH SOMBER OBJECTS LIKE DARK CANDLESTICKS, A VOLCANIC ROCK,
AND THE SKELETON OF A SMALL ANIMAL

(above)
SPARE DECORATIONS IN THE BEDROOM CONTRAST WITH THE REST OF
THE APARTMENT'S VISUAL BUSINESS, THOUGH THE GRAY WALLS PERPETUATE
THE SOBER MOOD

(overleaf left)
STEPHEN ALESCH STILL RENDERS BY HAND ON THIS ANTIQUE DRAFTING TABLE;
A SOFT BEARSKIN RUG CONTRASTS WITH THE HARDWOOD FLOOR

(overleaf right)
PAINTINGS, DRAWINGS, SCULPTURE, AND WOODEN FURNITURE FROM OTHER
ERAS FILL THE LOFT WITH HISTORY AND EMOTION

THE FOSHAY

MUNGE LEUNG

In August of 2008, the W Hotel Group sent out an electronic "telegram" announcing the imminent opening of its latest property, in Minneapolis, the Foshay. The typeset text asked, by way of introduction, "Who's ready to speakeasy?"

Built in the 1920s, the Foshay is a landmark building and was added to the U.S. National Register of Historic Places in 1978. This designation meant that the firm hired to renovate it, Munge Leung of Toronto, had to restore and preserve as much of the existing structure as they could in the process—one reason a Prohibition-inspired update made sense. The other was architect Alessandro Munge's interest in using Art Deco as a reaction to what he sees as the overuse of "cool-modern" in interiors.

An original, geometrically patterned terrazzo floor in the entryway introduces an X motif that is picked up and used in increasingly abstracted ways throughout the entire hotel. High-backed chairs scattered in public areas are covered with a tufted black leather that laces closed up the back—the seams illustrating one subtle instance of this theme.

The detailed metalwork of the lobby's fireplace and ornate large-filigree side tables is offset by the softness of a deep pile rug, its softness in turn offset by its own geometric pattern, the entire space a consistent loop of design and reference and experience. "We were after a sensuous warmth," Munge says. "We wanted guests to feel a connection to the history and culture of the structure."

Because of the Foshay's place in Minneapolis's cultural memory, the designers chose to retain many of the original details even if they were not technically protected by the landmark designation, and chose to enhance the historic elements where possible as well. The original, ornate elevator doors were burnished. Painted ceiling decorations were restored. In the second-floor ballroom, a digital mural pays homage to the state's history and uses imagery provided by the Minnesota Historical Society.

The hotel is a departure from many of the W brand's hotels, which focus mainly on contemporary furnishings and styles. Its recognition of, and careful attention to, today's new appreciation for old-time glamour signals that as a corporation, it recognizes the aesthetic possibilities of historical adoption.

(top)
STYLIZED WING CHAIRS IN THE ENTRY ARE A MODERN TWIST ON CLASSIC
HOTEL FURNITURE; THE ORIGINAL TERRAZZO FLOOR BEGINS A GEOMETRIC MOTIF USED
ELSEWHERE IN THE INTERIORS

(above)
FACETED GLASS DESKS GLOW IN THE RECEPTION AREA; A COMPLEMENTARY
PURPLE LIGHT EMANATES FROM THE RECESSED CEILING, ILLUMINATING THE ORIGINAL
ART DECO DETAILS

(previous pages)
SPARKLING STRANDS OF GLASS BEADS IN THE MAIN LOBBY FORM A COLUMN
OF LIGHT THAT CONTRASTS WITH THE DARK METAL OF THE ROLLED STEEL SCREEN
AND END TABLES

(above left)
RED LACQUER DRAWS ATTENTION TO THE LINES OF THIS COMPACT IN-ROOM BAR

(above right)
A STRIKING GEOMETRIC PATTERN MAKES THE BED POP AGAINST A GUEST
ROOM'S NEUTRAL TONES

(above left)
SLEEK STOOLS COZY UP TO A BAR; THE DARK INTERIOR REFERENCES THE
SPEAKEASY TRADITION

(above right)
A MURAL DEPICTING IMPORTANT MOMENTS IN MINNESOTA HISTORY PERPETUATES
THE FOSHAY'S PLACE IN THE AREA'S CULTURAL MEMORY

(above)
OVERSCALED FURNISHINGS INTRODUCE WHIMSY TO THE WEIGHTY
LANDMARK BUILDING

(opposite)
BRIGHT CHANDELIER LIGHT ILLUMINATES RESTORED CEILING DECORATIONS; STATELY
WOOD PANELS FRAME THE ENTRY TO THE HOTEL'S PROHIBITION BAR

(overleaf)
ROARING FLAMES—DIGITAL AS WELL AS REAL—AND CORSET-BACK CHAIRS OF
CAVALLINI COWHIDE CONTINUE THE BLEND OF TRADITIONAL AND CONTEMPORARY
ELEMENTS THAT DEFINE THE HOTEL'S PERSONALITY

APOTHEKE

CHRISTOPHER TIERNEY
HEATHER TIERNEY

On Manhattan's Doyers Street, a tiny elbow of a link between the short Pell Street and a history-laden stretch of the Bowery, an unassuming door leads to Apothéke, a bar that is one-third Parisian Belle Epoque–era absintherie, one-third eighteenth-century apothecary, and one-third Austrian champagne bar.

"I wasn't searching for this kind of place," owner Heather Tierney explains. "It found me." That sense of a different sort of agency, the feeling of being adopted by a place—rather than simply choosing a place—was what inspired Tierney and her brother Christopher, a designer, to create a space full of reference and history from different eras and places, ideals, and events. She believes New York's gritty and multicultural downtown is a fitting setting for a bar with three diverse influences.

The space is simply laid out but complexly detailed. A group of curved-back, green-like-absinthe, striped upholstery banquettes lines one exposed brick wall, while a 30-foot Carrera marble bar anchors the interior at its far end. The space is richly punctuated by a collection of old apothecary bottles and a series of backlit display arches that form their repository. The original ceiling was mainly left in its dilapidated condition to provide a direct counterpoint to the sleek, contemporary tile-inlaid floor. Armchair votives continue the sense of intimacy begun by the row of single-bulb wall sconces and velvet cubic ottomans.

The design is part of an overall ethos of environment change. The owners intend a trip to Apothéke to be a dose of medicine guaranteed to lift spirits or alter the human sensorium, and the result of their vision is an uncanny embodiment of the often subconscious reasons behind why people go out in the first place: for a change of scenery and to discover previously unimagined possibilities. Bartender Albert Trummer makes cocktails as fastidiously as a true pharmacist mixes drugs and "prescribes" particular drinks to "cure" various mood disorders; one wall is even decorated with chemical compound notations.

(above)
A BACKLIT MARBLE BAR COVERED WITH APOTHECARY BOTTLES
SALVAGED FROM A CHICAGO PHARMACY CONTRIBUTES TO THE DRINKS-AS-
PRESCRIPTIONS CONCEIT

(previous pages)
RECLAIMED WOOD COLUMNS AND SHEER CURTAINS DIVIDE THE MAIN
SPACE; STRIPED BANQUETTES PICK UP THE COLOR OF THE ABSINTHE-FILLED
GLOBES OF THE WALL SCONCES; THE MAIN CHANDELIER WAS DESIGNED
BY CHRISTOPHER TIERNEY

(above)
ROUND ARCHES ON THE BAR REDUCE THE ROOM'S PERCEIVED SCALE AND REPEAT THE
GRAPHIC MOTIF FOUND ELSEWHERE IN THE SPACE

(opposite)
AN EMBLEM REFERENCING THE CADUCEUS, ASSOCIATED WITH HEALING,
IS USED AS THE ESTABLISHMENT'S LOGO

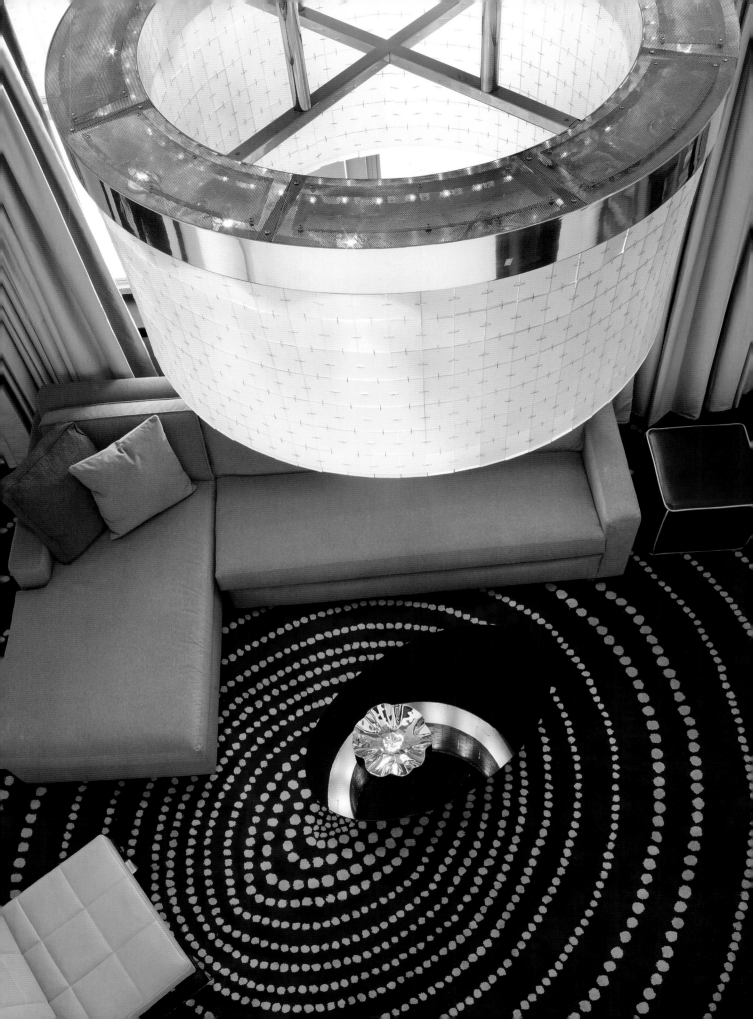

On the cusp of a global energy crisis, a small boutique hotel opened in the moneyed Texas city of Dallas. Funded by energy magnate Tim Headington, the Joule was designed by Transylvanian architect Adam Tihany around an idealized take on energy: what it means to us, how it is used, and what it looks like.

The shell of the hotel is a 1920s neo-Gothic bank building. Tihany's intervention is entirely rooted in the city and in the imaginations of its occupants. In Dallas, that means bigger and bolder. The lobby's centerpiece, a gigantic revolving gear, anchors the space, its slow and heavy motion an expression of the never-ending supply of energy produced in the state. This momentum is reiterated in the Charlie Palmer restaurant, where huge fans whir silently from the ceiling. Throughout, repeating geometric motifs of concentric circles are meant to remind visitors of electrical circuits and momentum.

It's all a romanticization of energy. The hotel is in no way particularly energy-efficient, or energy-focused, or sustainable. But it is luxurious, in a very specific and local sort of way. "It's a bit dark," Tihany says of the finishes and washes and colors—deep browns, dark purples, dusky suedes—that make up the walls and floors and furnishings of the relatively small 129-room hotel. "We couldn't really play on the luxury of space," he says. "Everything you touch is sleek and well made and elegant; it's a luxury of a different kind."

Energy, the design of the hotel argues, is something to be celebrated. This luxury hotel creates a poignant reminder of our cultural dependency on electricity and the ease it provides for our modern lives, but allows us to revel in it temporarily.

(above)
CEILING FANS MEANT TO EVOKE WIND TURBINES CONTINUE THE THEME OF CIRCLES,
GEARS, AND ENERGY USED THROUGHOUT THE HOTEL

(previous page, left)
IN A SUITE, THE CIRCULAR PATTERN OF THE RUG MAKES REFERENCE TO THE
ATOM AND THE MOVEMENT OF ELECTRONS AROUND A NEUTRON, PICKING UP THE
ENERGY THEME

(previous page, right)
CHANDELIERS OF CLEAR BEADS SUSPENDED FROM THIN STRINGS REFRACT LIGHT
IN ALLURING WAYS IN THE HOTEL'S BALLROOM

(above)
A MUTED PALETTE OF BURNT ORANGES AND DUSKY PURPLES IS ENLIVENED
WITH A GIANT ZEBRA-PRINT OTTOMAN

(opposite)
GLOBES ON THE SIDEBOARD BEGIN A MOTIF OF DIFFERENT SHAPES IN VERTICAL
COLUMNS REPEATED ON THE BACKDROP, LAMPS, AND RUG

(overleaf)
A MASSIVE STYLIZED GEAR REVOLVES SLOWLY IN THE MAIN LOBBY
FURNISHED WITH VELVET COUCHES IN SUBTLE TONES; AN ETCHED GLASS SCREEN
TO THE RIGHT PROVIDES SEPARATION FROM AN ELEVATOR BANK

Municipal buildings and government bureaucracy are unexpected sources of inspiration for an up-and-coming design and concept firm. But AvroKO's principals Greg Bradshaw, William Harris, Kristina O'Neal, and Adam Farmerie often find insight in unconventional places.

Public was one of the first New York restaurants to play with an aesthetic of reinterpreted nostalgia, and it became a touchstone for historically informed adaptive reuse—the pleasure of the reclaimed barn door, the brightly dropped filament bulb. "It's about not making things too precious," Harris says. "Many designers can get very wrapped up in quote-unquote 'design.'"

The firm owns and operates the restaurant, giving it complete control over everything from the design to the menu, created and cooked by Brad Farmerie, brother of Adam. The firm researched elements that would evoke municipal institutions past. The designers looked to ideas of collective memory as articulated through a public library and the thrill of discovery inherent in its card catalogs, and used them to archive every menu ever created at the restaurant. To re-create the intimacy of smaller, close-knit communities where grocers knew and made recommendations to their patrons, they introduced a wine-tasting system that "delivers" hand-selected bottles of wine to individually rented vintage post office boxes that line one wall of the restaurant.

AvroKO embraced the space's industrial rawness, and by day the restaurant's two main dining areas—one upstairs and refined, dressed with bright white lamps and a row of crisply set tables, one downstairs and grittier, detailed with exposed brick and a piece of taxidermy—look spare and airy. At night, however, filament bulbs glow, brick darkens, and the space becomes the perfect setting for traditional, hearty standards like oxtail ravioli and sticky toffee pudding.

The detail expressed in Public, in the consistency of design from the typewriter typography of the menus to the obviously government-issue doors, the hanging mailbox keys with their rubber-stamp labels, and the books with their Dewey decimal–inspired classifications lining the coat check space, creates an unexpected but familiar sense of honesty.

(top)
VINTAGE POST OFFICE BOXES LINE THE ENTRYWAY

(above)
DELICATE FILAMENT BULBS AND HARDY METAL LAMPS SUSPENDED FROM A BEAMED
CEILING VARY THE INTENSITY OF LIGHT IN THE ROOM

(previous pages)
INDUSTRIAL DETAILS—BARE BULBS, A SLIDING GARAGE-STYLE DOOR, EXPOSED
BRICK, METAL STOOLS—VIE WITH SCULPTED SEATING AND CRISPLY OUTLINED TABLES
IN THE CASUAL DOWNSTAIRS DINING AREA

(above)
A SLEEK LIGHTBOX ILLUMINATES THE UPSTAIRS DINING AREA AND ITS
RECLAIMED BARN DOOR

(opposite)
FORMER LIBRARY BOOKS SIT ATOP A CARD CATALOG THAT HOUSES THE
RESTAURANT'S MENU ARCHIVES; PURPOSEFULLY STIFF, FORMAL CHAIRS CREATE
A SMALL READING AREA

BOBO
CARLOS SUAREZ
DEKAR DESIGN

There was a brief New York moment when it seemed that the bigger and shinier a restaurant, the better. The year of Bobo's opening, 2006, was also the year of the big-box joint, when celebrity chefs introduced sprawling three-hundred-seat spaces that even star designers struggled to humanize. Intimacy was relegated to the smaller establishments, the hidden bars, places where reservations were a must.

Until Carlos Suarez escaped from restaurant giant B. R. Guest and decided to open something a little more snug, something that would operate as an antithesis to what he saw as the impersonal and uninteresting standards being promoted all over town. Spread over three floors of an unsigned townhouse in Manhattan's West Village neighborhood, Bobo, the name a shortening of the term "bourgeois bohemian," is a helter-skelter hodgepodge of furniture trucked in and installed by Suarez, his cousin Dolores Suarez of Dekar Design, and her partner Caroline Grant. Photographs of his actual family dot the walls.

"You feel like you're in a home," Suarez says, explaining his decision to embrace personal touches. "The idea was that I'd inherited this great apartment in Paris form an eccentric uncle, and with it I inherited his family photos, books, furniture, and fixtures." Dekar's background in residential design helped realize the feeling of stumbling into an enthusiastic host's home.

The entrance leads down a few steps and through a typical apartment door into a low-ceilinged, exposed-brick bar dining area, complete with miniature organ and books piled high on the mantel. Deep leather banquettes and armchairs provide close-comfort seating, and the ceiling's exposed wood beams reinforce the historical mood. Upstairs, the main dining room has been architecturally divided into three distinct zones: a library, a proper formal dining room to the front, and a looser casual corner to the back.

"I think people appreciate the human contact and the connection," Suarez explains. "They're over the fireworks and entertainment, and want something a little more satisfying." Spinning vinyl records in a restaurant that looks like a ritzy townhouse you happen to have stumbled into on a West Village corner is doing the trick.

(above)
PHOTOS OF SUAREZ'S FAMILY LINE ONE SIDE OF THE MAIN DINING ROOM;
MISMATCHED CHAIRS, TABLES AND BANQUETTES OF DIFFERENT SIZES,
AND AN ORNATE MIRROR ABOVE A BOOK-LINED MANTEL CREATE THE SENSE
THAT THE SPACE COULD BE SOMEONE'S HOME

(previous pages)
A MINIATURE ORGAN TAKES CENTER STAGE DOWNSTAIRS, WHILE EXPOSED
BRICKWORK ON THE WALLS AND BEAMS ON THE CEILING CONTRIBUTE TO THE
FEELING OF A HISTORIC INN

(overleaf)
MEMENTOS AND BOOKS LINE THE HEXAGONAL CUBBIES OF AN UNUSUAL
BOOKCASE, CONTINUING THE THEME OF AD-HOC CREATIVITY

SHOREDITCH HOUSE

TOM DIXON

This social club, designed by the London-based Tom Dixon in a Dickensian-era tea warehouse, introduced an older and vintage aesthetic to the wave of new private clubs in that city that started with the opening of SoHo House. Dixon, a Tunisian-born art school dropout who learned how to make furniture by first teaching himself how to weld—his first line was made out of salvaged pieces—and then by designing chairs for companies like Cappellini, brought a mix-and-match sensibility to his design for Shoreditch House.

The overall ethos is of upright but not uptight relaxation. This relationship between industrial roots and homelike comfort continues throughout Shoreditch; its darkly evocative background aesthetic is brought to light by contrasting it with a casual interspersion of poppy colors. While the blend of old and new elements begins in the simply appointed Biscuit Tin restaurant, where round-back armchairs pull up to a plain wood table and sculptural lamps and heating ducts take up equal space overhead, a more sophisticated but similar blend continues on the large upper floor.

The design coalesces in the Square Bar. Simple yet delicately curved tables anchor one side of the space, while a length of deep black tufted leather banquettes creates an invitation to stretch out on the other. Spare metal-and-leather stools are reflected in the bar, their muted colors echoing the heavy lamps and taps on top, their lines slipping into the rustic wood plank floor. In the main House Kitchen dining area, simple black chairs provide a consistent visual marker, while gigantic lamps enclose and delineate pockets of space.

Dixon's sense of play is reiterated in the Sitting Room, a large space dotted with high-backed chairs in alternating black and pink, plushly upholstered to contrast with the spare ceiling. Hanging corset-shaped lamps and spare wrought-iron chandeliers reference bygone centuries. Modernity is introduced with sleek coffee tables and geometric white bookshelves. The many contrasts between soft and hard, shiny and matte, and plush and smooth give this space its lively energy.

(top)
COMFORTABLE SEATS IN BLACK AND DARK PEACOCK BLUE LEATHER
BECKON IN THE SQUARE BAR

(above)
DIXON'S WELDING-INFLUENCED AESTHETIC IS ILLUSTRATED IN THE HOUSE
KITCHEN'S HALF-MOON LAMPS

(previous pages)
THE SITTING ROOM COMBINES BRIGHT COLORS WITH NOSTALGIC
SHAPES IN THE FORM OF PINK WING CHAIRS AND GEOMETRIC BOOKSHELVES,
A CONTRAST THAT CONTINUES WITH AN EXPOSED CEILING FROM WHICH
DELICATE CORSET-SHAPED LIGHTS HANG

(above)
HIGHLY POLISHED BRASS REFLECTS LIGHT THROUGHOUT THE BAR

(opposite)
TRADITIONAL FURNITURE SHAPES AND OLD-FASHIONED GAMES
ARE GIVEN A CONTEMPORARY TREATMENT IN THE SITTING ROOM

(overleaf)
A MASSIVE MODERN CHANDELIER IN THE MAIN RECEPTION AREA ADDS A
LAYER OF TEXTURE TO THE WHITE-PAINTED BRICK WALLS, SPARE WINDOW FRAMES,
AND PLUSH UPHOLSTERY

BROOKLYN TOWNHOUSE

JENNA LYONS
VINCENT MAZEAU

This Brooklyn townhouse was a wreck when its current owners discovered it: a jumble of unattractive linoleum floors, carved-up rooms, crooked stairs, and dark hallways. The aim of artist Vincent Mazeau and creative director Jenna Lyons was to restore the three-story house to how it might conceivably have looked, had its original layout and details been more carefully preserved.

"We wanted the actual architectural details of the house to look original, and like only the furniture was brought in," Lyons says, standing on the wide, rough, unpolished planks (brought in) that make up the floor of their sunny kitchen, her coffee cup resting on a marked-up concrete countertop (brought in), near a long and dripped-on table (brought in) that anchors the bright and airy space. For the couple, the house's memory lies deeply entrenched in their imaginations.

"The best compliment is when people look at the floor and say, 'Oh, you're going to keep it like this?'" Mazeau says. They rescued planks from an old New Hampshire barn and carefully calibrated their exact placement to have cracks and holes in certain visible places to maximize the sense of authenticity. Similarly, the front hall was left unstained to create a look that was worn, spotted, and weathered. Heavy marble fireplaces in the living/dining room look like they were installed when the house was first built—only a close observer would suspect that these antiques were a later addition, since they do not actually match.

Upstairs the perceived restoration continues. A raised bathtub takes center stage in a nook just off the master bedroom, its dark glossiness framed by a detailed gray arch that appears to be original to the structure. Actually, the arch is one of the few architectural interventions performed by the couple. A hand-troweled concrete wall lends the room a sense of industrial chic. The house's lighting ties everything together: mercury bulb sconces illuminate the small downstairs bathroom and a smoky orb inserted into the ceiling's original plaster medallion illumines the upstairs. It's all a bit old, a bit off, and it fits perfectly into the neighborhood's cycle of history and renovation.

(above left)
A DARK ARCHWAY LEADS FROM THE MASTER BEDROOM TO THE BATH, WHERE A CLAW-FOOT
TUB PAINTED IN A DARK SHEEN RESTS ON RECLAIMED WOOD PLANK FLOORING

(above right)
STAINLESS STEEL APPLIANCES ECHO THE KITCHEN'S INDUSTRIAL AESTHETIC OF ROUGH
CONCRETE COUNTERTOPS AND SALVAGED FLOOR PLANKS

(previous page, left)
A YELLOW COUCH ADDS A BIT OF BRIGHTNESS IN A LIVING ROOM OF OTHERWISE DARK
FURNISHINGS AND FINISHES—GRAY WALLS, BLACK LEATHER CHAIRS, A ZEBRA RUG AND
FUR THROWS, AND AN ORNATE CHANDELIER FITTED WITH BLACK CANDLESTICKS

(previous page, right)
A COLLECTION OF ANTLERS FROM AROUND THE WORLD IS ASSEMBLED ON ONE WALL;
ART, INCLUDING A PALLET MADE BY MAZEAU, SURROUNDS THE ANTIQUE FIREPLACE

LA ESQUINA

SERGE BECKER
DEREK SANDERS

At the vertex of a triangle of SoHo streets, a bright neon sign announces The Corner, with a subtitle reading "La Esquina." The metal-clad sliver of a building looks like a transplanted Los Angeles taco cart, its fold-up shutters and Jarritos soda–filled windows a direct replica of owner Serge Becker's beloved West Coast taquerias. The takeout restaurant is bright, busy, and cheap. But that's just the front.

Through a door marked Employees Only, past a gatekeeper who might be either purposefully sullen or helpfully friendly—depending on the day, the mood, and the restaurant's capacity—a set of narrow and twisted stairs leads through a bright-white, cook-filled kitchen, a moment of over stimulation that ends with entry to the downstairs restaurant, a cavern of exposed brick and dark wood furniture, expressive lamps, and warrenlike secrecy.

Becker is an impresario of hidden bars and emotion-filled spaces, and opening the restaurant was, for him, a response to the anodyne modernism of New York's architectural landscape. Becker, who worked with architect Derek Sanders, wanted to create a space in which his design directed people to behave in certain ways: to let their guards down, to feel possibility, and to connect with each other.

"It's like painting using light and mood and atmosphere," Becker says. "I'm always proud when I can do it with the least number of brush strokes." The interventions here are a mix of faux discoveries and clear introductions. After years of disappointment in craftsmen and contractors who couldn't quite interpret plans the way he envisioned, Becker embraced the fault lines of the human hand evident in the realization of La Esquina. Uneven wood planks and doors that are almost too heavy to push are, here, perfect in their imperfections. In the neighboring café, which Becker opened as a way of inviting the neighborhood into the world of La Esquina without necessarily inviting everyone through the secret door, Becker ended up repainting fake flakes onto the wall; his request for workers to scrape just some of it off in order to give it a worn look had been carried out over enthusiastically, and the restaurateur had to actually add a layer to create a look of loss.

Constant tension between creation and removal makes La Esquina an evocative restaurant. It is at once a secret that everyone knows about, a trustworthy home, and a marker of an outsized reality.

(above)
AN ABRUPT SHIFT IN MATERIALS AND MOOD MARKS THE POINT
AT WHICH THE KITCHEN ENDS AND THE UNDERGROUND RESTAURANT
LA ESQUINA BEGINS

(previous pages)
A MOSAIC COMBINING BECKER'S FASCINATION WITH CARS AND MEXICAN
ART GREETS VISITORS

(above left)
THE LOW, VAULTED CEILING OF THIS WARREN OF A RESTAURANT IS ECHOED
BY THE CURVE OF THE BANQUETTE AND ILLUMINATED BY EERIE CANDLESTICKS

(above right)
A STILL-LIFE-WORTHY FRUIT BOWL PROVIDES A MOMENT OF CONDENSED
CLARITY WITHIN THIS SHADOW-SATURATED ATMOSPHERE

(opposite)
WOODEN CHAIRS, ROUGHLY PAINTED BRICK WALLS, HEAVY WOOD PLANKS, AND
A CABINET COVERED IN CHICKEN WIRE REFERENCE RURAL FARMS

(above)
OMINOUS METAL SCREENS DIVIDE THE BAR FROM THE DINING AREA

(opposite)
ORNATE GLASS LAMPS AND MELTING CANDLES SPOTLIGHT SECTIONS OF
THE MAIN BAR; THE AESTHETIC OF GRITTY FLOOR PLANKS IS PICKED UP AGAIN
BY THE BARSTOOLS

New York Times reporter Denny Lee called it "Mr. Schrager's obituary for cold minimalism." *Travel + Leisure* referred to the aesthetic as "haute bohemian." The Gramercy Park Hotel, Ian Schrager's landmark property, is another arrow in the quiver of decoration and ornament, its rococo appreciation of things we want to touch and its art-influenced creation of lobby walls we want to look at a reinterpretation and reconfiguration of the hotel's beloved past.

First opened in 1925, the original Gramercy Park Hotel, on the corner of New York's only private park, was over the 1920s and 1930s home to characters like the literary critic Edmund Wilson and the novelist Mary McCarthy. From the 1950s, when it was bought by New York hotel owner Herbert Weissberg, through 2003, when hotelier-of-the-nineties Ian Schrager bought it, the hotel saw visitors like Madonna and the Clash, and residents like James Cagney and David Mamet. All these people have given the hotel a sense of social history, have lent their own histories to these halls and rooms and bars. Schrager hired the brilliant conceptual artist Julian Schnabel to do the interiors. The man who famously painted an entire West Village building pink used that same sense of rambunctious play in the design and architecture here.

The lobby opens onto a carpet, the letters GPH purposefully haphazard—unequally spaced and sized, their outlines wobbly—scrawled onto a red rug that weaves its ornamented way through the space, creating a plush contrast to the black-and-white checkerboard floor. Gigantic rough wood columns with square shapes are at purposeful odds with the delicacy of much of the space's fine-grained detail, like the fringed and upholstered chairs. A mix of lighting fixtures from different eras creates a sense of warm luxury. The rooms themselves continue this bohemian aesthetic with daring color combinations of purest cobalt blue and shocking reds, and fearless furniture—tassels! In 2006! Schnabel designed the beds, with their detailing evocative of Victorian traveling trunks, himself.

Part of the Gramercy Park Hotel's history is real, but much of it is embellished by our imaginations. The combination of bold color and unconventional furniture used here brings the hotel's design forward, making a provocative statement about the reembrace of decoration, articulation, and fancy.

(above)
IN A TYPICAL GUEST ROOM SATURATED WITH COLOR, A VELVET ARMCHAIR
AND OTTOMAN SIT ACROSS FROM A BED INSPIRED BY THE LOOK OF A
VICTORIAN TRUNK; A VINTAGE-INSPIRED LAMP SITS ATOP A SIDE TABLE WITH AN
INTRICATELY EMBROIDERED TOP

(previous pages)
THE ROSE BAR'S TILED FLOOR PROVIDES A STARK GEOMETRIC CONTRAST
TO THE ORGANIC SHAPES OF THE SHELVING; A SINGLE ABSTRACTED HISTORICAL
ORNAMENT IS REINVENTED AS A MURAL

(overleaf)
CURVED SHAPES APPEAR AGAIN IN THE JADE BAR, THIS TIME CUT INTO A
GRAINY WOOD WALL; FRINGE ON DEEP BLUE STOOLS INTRODUCES A SENSE OF
WHIMSY AND HISTORY

(top)
TEDDY BEAR'S PICNIC BY ARTIST/DESIGNER JULIAN SCHNABEL PUNCTUATES
THE FAR WALL IN THE ROSE BAR

(above)
IN THE MAIN LOBBY SPACE, A GESTURAL CY TWOMBLY ADDS MODERNITY
TO THE HEAVY COFFERED CEILING, VELVET UPHOLSTERY, AND WROUGHT-IRON
FIREPLACE ACCESSORIES

(opposite)
A MODERN USE OF HISTORICAL ORNAMENT APPEARS AGAIN WOVEN
INTO THE RUG, EMBROIDERED ON CHAIR BACKS, AND IN A TONGUE-IN-CHEEK
USE OF TRIMMINGS

CAFE WA S

JASON VOLENEC

RKIT DESIGN

Los Angeles is a city known for the recency and brightness of its architecture, for its low-slung and relatively easy-going Art Deco nature and urbanist design. This makes it all the more remarkable that Ivan Kane, the man behind the Forty Deuce burlesque club, wanted to introduce whimsical history, in the form of a restaurant that felt as if it had been around for a hundred years, to Hollywood. Jason Volenec realized the irrationality and appeal of that desire in such a new city, and capitalized on it.

Translating Kane's unusual wish for a space that would feel as though it had been only recently rediscovered into architecture meant Volenec had to address this logical fallacy and embrace it. "It would be much more human if it was irrational," Volenec explains. And so, in the café, stories are begun grandly but never quite finished. Doors disappear into the floor; paintings into the ceiling; a grand staircase leads to nowhere. Even the name was derived from the space's original imperfect sign—it originally proclaimed "Café Always Open" but had been reduced to "Café _ _ wa_s Open" over the years as the neon bulbs eventually gave out.

In the same way that replicas—even when honestly and thoughtfully and subtly carried out—are usually removed enough from originals to be obvious reproductions, Café Wa s had the potential to veer too far into ironic territory, to become a spoof rather than theater, a skit rather than a play. Volenec, however, stopped the story one moment shy of the point where disbelief would make its entrance, tactfully adding just enough period details to make the space plausible.

The final decor makes it apparent that the designer knew exactly what the owner was after. Kane is so thrilled with the space that he spends as much time as possible there. It is fitting that in this city of stage sets, movie magic, and illusion, a piano bar so self-consciously styled feels right at home.

(above)
A CARPETED STAIRCASE MYSTERIOUSLY LEADS TO NOWHERE

(previous pages)
A PAINTING HUNG ON THE CEILING AND PARTIALLY OBSCURED
BY THICK RED CURTAINS INTRODUCES SURREALISM TO THIS MIRROR-LINED
PRIVATE DINING AREA

(above)
SELF-AWARE REFERENCE CONTINUES WITH TELEVISIONS PLASTERED
OVER WITH PRINT

(opposite)
BOOKS AND CANDLES DRAW THE EYE TOWARD A HALF-FRAMED,
SIDEWAYS PAINTING

(above)
THE EARLY TWENTIETH CENTURY COMES ALIVE WITH ORNATE LIGHT FIXTURES,
HEAVY PATTERNED CURTAINS, AND WOODEN FURNISHINGS IN THE BALCONY'S BAR

(opposite)
DARK WOODS AND VELVET-COVERED STOOLS ADD NOSTALGIC WARMTH TO
A BAR THAT SLOWLY REVEALS SURREAL DETAILS SUCH AS PAINTINGS THAT EMERGE
ONLY PARTIALLY FROM THE CEILING AND PIANO KEYS DETACHED FROM THE
ORIGINAL INSTRUMENT

(following pages)
A CHUNKY COLUMN COVERED IN CONTRASTING LAYERS OF WALLPAPER—ONE RIPPED
AND DELFT-INSPIRED, THE OTHER A JUVENILE WESTERN PRINT OF HORSES AND
LASSOES—REQUIRES A SECOND GLANCE